Kentucky Bourbon Whiskey

KENTUCKY BOURBON WHISKEY

AN AMERICAN HERITAGE

Michael R. Veach

UNIVERSITY PRESS OF KENTUCKY

Copyright © 2013 by The University Press of Kentucky

Scholarly publisher for the Commonwealth,
serving Bellarmine University, Berea College, Centre College of
Kentucky, Eastern Kentucky University, The Filson Historical Society,
Georgetown College, Kentucky Historical Society, Kentucky State
University, Morehead State University, Murray State University,
Northern Kentucky University, Transylvania University, University of
Kentucky, University of Louisville, and Western Kentucky University.
All rights reserved.

Editorial and Sales Offices: The University Press of Kentucky
663 South Limestone Street, Lexington, Kentucky 40508–4008
www.kentuckypress.com

17 16 15 14 13   5 4 3 2 1

Cataloging-in-Publication data is available from the Library of
Congress.

ISBN 978-0-8131-4165-7 (hardcover : alk. paper)
ISBN 978-0-8131-4171-8 (epub)
ISBN 978-0-8131-4172-5 (pdf)

This book is printed on acid-free paper meeting the requirements of
the American National Standard for Permanence in Paper for Printed
Library Materials.

Manufactured in the United States of America.

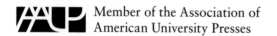
Member of the Association of
American University Presses

Dedicated to my father, James Veach,
and my nephew, Bryon Veach.
I wish they both could have seen
the finished product.

Contents

Preface   ix

1. Farmer Distillers and the Whiskey Rebellion   3

2. The Origin of Bourbon Whiskey   19

3. The Industrial Revolution and the Distilling Industry   31

4. Distillers and Rectifiers   45

5. Taxation and Regulation   63

6. Prohibition and the Bourbon Industry   77

7. The End of Prohibition and the Second World War   91

8. Boom and Then Bust   105

9. Into the Twenty-first Century   113

Acknowledgments   125

Notes   127

Bibliography   131

Index   135

Preface

This book has been twenty years in the making. In the summer of 1991 I was a graduate student at the University of Louisville studying medieval history with a secondary field of public history. I had done an internship at the Filson Historical Society and was due to do another one in the 1991–1992 academic year. That is when Dr. Nicholas Morgan from United Distillers (UD) called the History Department looking for a graduate student to create an archive from some papers and artifacts at the Stitzel-Weller Distillery. The job was to last six thirty-five-hour weeks and pay $9.00 an hour. Needless to say, the offer was attractive, and I accepted. The job eventually turned into a full-time position that lasted until the end of 1996, when UD sold its bourbon brands and closed the archive.

As a native Kentuckian, I thought I knew a lot about bourbon whiskey, but soon after taking the UD archive job I realized how wrong I was. From my work with the archive I learned the basics of the history of bourbon. I also had excellent teachers in my Stitzel-Weller colleagues Ed Foote, Mike Wright, and Chris Morris. Ed taught me how bourbon was fermented, distilled, and aged; Mike what makes a good bourbon good and a bad bourbon bad; and Chris how to market bourbon and create new brands.

While working at the UD archive I came in contact with many other people in the industry. Al Young at Four Roses in particular began to come hear me any time I gave a talk on bourbon history. A friendship soon grew, and knowledge was exchanged. I also began a working relationship with the two curators of the Oscar Getz Museum of Whiskey History, Flaget Nally and Mary Hite, who were a wealth of knowledge about the museum collection and distilling in general, Mary's father and grandfather having both been accomplished distillers, and Flaget having worked in the industry before joining the Getz staff. Thanks to my museum connection I was able to curate a number of exhibitions drawing on the UD collection and also to help organize the Bourbon Heritage Panel and the Master Distiller's Auction as part of the museum's Kentucky Bourbon Festival.

In 1997 I found myself unemployed, and Jim Holmberg at the Filson Historical Society hired me as a special collections assistant. I continued to work with bourbon history, kept up my connection with the Getz Museum and the Kentucky Bourbon Festival, and fielded questions about bourbon history from the many callers who had received my number from one of the distilleries. I also did some consulting work for several distilleries and contributed to bourbonenthusiast.com and other websites.

In 2006 the Kentucky Distillers' Association made me a member of the Kentucky Bourbon Hall of Fame as a historian of the industry. This led Laura Sutton of the University Press of Kentucky to contact me in the spring of 2007 about writing this book. She convinced me that the book needed to be done and that it need not be abstruse or exhaustive. She pointed out that there was not a history of the industry in print and that a good survey would be well received. That is what I have attempted to provide.

The history of the bourbon industry is a rich one that mirrors the history of America. The Whiskey Rebellion reflected the troubles that the newly united states had coalescing under a federal government. The whiskey tax, which sparked the rebellion, was the first federal tax and prefigured all others, especially the federal income tax. The changes wrought by the Industrial Revolution can be seen as the modernization of distilling technology writ large. Even the general health of the bourbon industry mirrors that of the country as a whole, declining in bad economic and social times and reviving in good times. This book discusses all this and more. As noted, it cannot be, and is not meant to be, exhaustive. I will consider it a success if it simply leads the reader to a better understanding of the bourbon industry. Perhaps it will also inspire others to further explore the territory I have opened.

KENTUCKY BOURBON WHISKEY

1

Farmer Distillers and the Whiskey Rebellion

Spirits were distilled in America long before the birth of the whiskey industry. Rum and gin were produced in cities along the Eastern Seaboard by colonists who had brought their stills with them to the New World. Whiskey came into widespread favor only with the end of the Revolutionary War and the beginning of the westward expansion, when the costs of transporting the ingredients over the mountains made rum and gin too expensive to produce. Whiskey could, however, be made from readily available local produce, and it became one of the most common of the home-produced spirits. In the early years of the westward expansion, stills were still manufactured in the East, and settlers had to bring them west with them. But demand soon grew large enough that coppersmiths began to manufacture them in western Pennsylvania and Kentucky.

The American pot still differed little from the European still, which had been in use for centuries. It was simply a large copper pot made to be fitted with a separate head and goose-

The Worm

The "worm" of an early pot still is a copper tube coming off the head of the still that is coiled through a barrel of water to help cool and condense the vapors coming off the still. The invention of the worm is often credited to the Germans. It is this innovation that makes the production of spirits practical. The worm cools the alcohol vapors, causing them to condense into liquid form.

neck that could be attached to the copper worm, a coil of copper tubing immersed in a barrel of water. The fermented mash, or "distiller's beer," which was made from grain, was poured into the pot, and the head was positioned on top of the pot and sealed to prevent the vapors from leaking through the joint. The beer was heated over an open fire, allowing the alcohol to vaporize and pass through the worm, where the water cooled the vapors, which became liquid again, allowing the alcohol to be collected and stored in a cistern. The whiskey could then be refined and made more palatable by distilling it a second time—in either the same still or a second still called a *doubler*—refining the quality of the spirit by taking out unpleasant flavors. The end result was clear, unflavored liquid alcohol. Color and taste came from the fruit, sugar, or herbs added after distillation.

Because the stills most of these farmers possessed needed to be easy to transport, they were rarely over 150 gallons in capacity. Their output was therefore limited—never more than 1,000 gallons a year and sometimes less than 100. The still

Pot stills at the Harlan Distillery in Monroe County, Kentucky, 1918. This photograph could have been taken in 1818, as the technology remained the same a century later. (Courtesy United Distillers Archive)

described by Henry Clay in an undated copy of a court document filed in Kentucky's Fayette County Court on behalf of his cousin Green Clay—Green Clay had in October 1800 purchased a still from George Coons and John Cock that had never been delivered—is typical. It is described as follows: "one still to hold one hundred and fifteen gallons exclusive of the cap, and has a cap and worm with the still." This is an average size for a still. It is large enough that beer from two fifty-gallon fermenting tubs can be distilled in it. Clay goes on to indicate that the still "should be of good thick copper, such as was common for a still of that size and to be finished off in a good workmanlike manner, with lead where the arm joins the cap and the spout."[1] Such construction would guarantee many years of use.

Farmers in the newly opened territories looked at distilled alcohol the same way they looked at salted pork and smoked hams—as just another product to sell, whether in jugs or barrels, for cash or barter for needed goods and services. A farm-based distillery was usually a small-time operation, typically one or two stills with a capacity of about one hundred gallons each. The beer a farmer distilled was made from grain he raised. Farmers who did not own stills often used a neighbor's, paying for use with a portion of the whiskey produced. Millers too distilled whiskey. Because they kept a portion of the grain they milled as payment, they always had a surplus on hand that could be turned to profit. And many millers turned this surplus grain into whiskey, which was more valuable than grain because it was easier to transport.

Early distillers made their whiskey from whatever grain they had on hand—usually corn or rye but also occasionally wheat. An example of an early recipe (ca. 1800) for mash bill (the ingredients from which the fermented mash is distilled) is the "Pennington Method":

PENNINGTON METHOD stilling

Take 12 gallons of boiling water Put into a tub then put in one 1 bus'l corn meal and steer well go over three tubs in this manner Then begin at the first tub & put into it 10 or 12 gallons of boiling water in each then stir as above Then fill your still again with water to boil—20 minutes after this put 4 gallons cold water to each tub then add one gallon of malt add to this half bus'l rye meal stir these all together well when the still boils add ten gallons boiling water to each tub Stir as aforsaid, Then let your tubs stand ab't 3 or 4 hours after which fill up your tubs with cold water Stir as above then let the Tubs stand until as warm as milk or rather cooler then yeast them.[2]

This is typical of recipes for mash bill that have survived from the late eighteenth century and the early nineteenth. Early distillers made either "sweet mash" or "sour mash" whiskey. Making a sweet mash involved simply cooking the grain and adding yeast to make the beer. The Pennington Method is an example of a sweet mash. A sour mash was made by using some of the liquid from a previous distillation in the new mash. This process ensured consistency between batches by creating an environment favorable to the particular yeast strain flavoring the whiskey. It also made that mash more acidic, preventing bacterial infection.

One of the earliest surviving recipes for sour mash dates

The Harlan Distillery mash tubs, 1918. (Courtesy United Distillers Archive)

Wort or Mash?

Scotch whiskey is distilled from a "wort," while bourbon whiskey is distilled from a "mash." A wort is made by cooking the grains and draining the sugary liquid off before fermentation, leaving the solids behind. A mash leaves the grain meal in the liquid during the fermenting process. Since pot stills have to be cleaned between every distillation, the fewer solids involved in distillation, the better. Grain solids will harden in the still, making it more difficult to clean. Modern bourbon is made with a continuous still, and mash flows through the column without interruption, washing the solids to the bottom of the still, where they become part of the spent beer.

to 1818 and is attributed to one Catherine Carpenter of Casey County, Kentucky, who continued to run her husband's distillery after his death. She recorded her recipes for both sweet mash and sour mash:

RECEIPT FOR DISTILLING CORN MEAL SWEET MASH

To a hundred gallon tub put in a bushel and a half of hot water then a half a bushel of meal Stir it well then one bushel of water; then a half bushel of meal & amp; so no untill you have mashed one bushel and a half of corn meal—Stir it all effectively then sprinkle a double handful of meal over the mash let it stand two hours then pour over the mash 2 gallons of warm water put in a half gallon of malt stir that well into the mash then stir in a half a bushel of Rye or wheat meal. Stir it well for 15 minutes put in another half gallon of malt. Stir it well and very frequently untill you can bear your hand in the mash up to your wrist then put in three bushels of cold slop or one gallon of good yeast then fill up with cold water. If you use yeast put in the cold water first and then the yeast. If you have neither yeast or Slop put in three peck of Beer from the bottom of a tub.

RECEIPT FOR DISTILLING BY A SOUR MASH

Put into the mash tub Six busheles of very hot slop then put in one Bushel of corn meal ground pretty course Stir well then sprinkle a little meal over the mash let it stand 5 days that is 3 full days betwist the Day you mash and the day you cool off—on the fifth day put in 3 gallons of warm water then put in one gallon of rye meal and one gallon of malt work it well into the malt and stir for 3 quarters of an hour then fill the tub half full of Luke warm water. Stir it well and with a fine sieve or otherwise Break all the lumps fine then let stand for three hours then fill up the tub with luke warm water.

For warm weather—five bushels of slop instead of six let it stand an hour and a half

Instead of three hours and cold water instead of warm.[3]

Because the quality of the whiskey they produced was inconsistent, farmers used other methods to improve its taste, such as flavoring it with fruit to make cordials or herbs to make gin. There are many recipes from early nineteenth-century Kentucky for making blackberry cordial or cherry "bounce" from whiskey. Cherry bounce—a form of flavored whiskey made from local ingredients—was a popular spirit in early Kentucky. It was intended both for personal use and for sale to others. The Beall-Booth Family Papers of the Filson Historical Society offer these recipes from the first decade of the nineteenth century:

Cordials—To one gallon of finished whiskey add two quarts of clear water. Then add about 30 Drops of the oil of cloves and five or six drops of the oil of Aniss Seed in a sufficient quantity of Sirup to sweeten it—Gin may be made by adding about 25 drops of the oil of juniper to each gallon.

Receipt to make Cherry Bounce of finished whiskey. Take the bark of the root of the wild cherry tree and steep it in hot water till it becomes strong then add such proportions of it as is sufficient to give it the cherry taste. Take care to have it high colored and sweetened with sirup.

Another method of finishing whiskey for consumption was to filter it through charcoal. The charcoal would remove many of the unpleasant-tasting fusel oils (nonethanol alcohols produced by the yeast as well as nonalcohol flavors in the spirits) that were left after distillation. It would also neutralize some of the natural acids in the alcohol, making it sweeter. The Beall-Booth Family Papers also give us a description of charcoal filtering:

Receipt to purify whisky and other Ardent Spirits. Take a tub of one hundred gallons and put a false Bottom about 8 or 10 inches from the other bottom the false bottom must be full of Holes then fasten on the top of the false bottom three or four thicknesses of white flannel then put about three or four inches thick clean white sand then put about 18 or 20 Inches thick of pulverized charcoal made of good green wood such as sugar tree Hickory & then fill up the vacancy with whisky or other ardent spirits take care to pour it up til it becomes perfectly clear and purified. To make Rum add one to five [i.e. one to five runs through the filter] Brandy one to four or five.

This process is similar to the "Lincoln County Process" used by Jack Daniel's Distillery and George Dickel's Cascade Hollow Distillery to make their Tennessee whiskey. The main difference is that, in the modern Tennessee whiskey distillery, the tub is taller and holds more charcoal, allowing the distiller to run the whiskey through fewer times.

At about the same time that whiskey came into favor with distillers, taxes came into favor with legislators. The requisite two-thirds of the original thirteen colonies had ratified the Constitution of the new United States by the summer of 1788, clearing the way for the creation of the new federal government. The most important thing distinguishing this new government from the much weaker one created by the Articles of Confederation was its ability to levy taxes nationwide. Because the new government had assumed the debts incurred by the pursuance of the Revolutionary War and the operation of the Confederation government, it needed money. To raise it, it established a number of taxes and tariffs, including an excise tax on whiskey and other distilled spirits in 1791.

The whiskey tax was promoted by the secretary of the Treasury, Alexander Hamilton, and his supporters. The designers of the tax wanted to move the economy away from cottage industries and into an industrialized economy. In theory the tax was fair to all producers, but in reality it favored the larger producers along the Atlantic coast. For one thing, it was to be paid in hard currency, and there was a shortage of coinage of any type in the frontier West. In the largely barter economy that prevailed there, whiskey itself became a substitute currency, and farmers traded it for supplies and even land. The larger distilleries in the coastal cities had greater access to currency since they most often sold their product for cash.

The government's dual standard for tax collection also favored the big distilleries. In urban areas, a tax collector could monitor production and tax the amount of the spirit actually produced. Those distillers who lived in areas that "the law defined as the country," as William Hogeland put it in his history of the Whiskey Rebellion, were treated differently.[4] The capacity of their stills was gauged, full-time production was assumed, and a tax equivalent to four months' production was assessed. Because farmers rarely distilled more than two months a year and sometimes as little as one week a year, they were being charged taxes for whiskey they would never produce.

Efforts to collect the whiskey tax in the frontier West met with resistance. Some tax collectors even found themselves tarred and feathered. In September 1792, President Washington issued a proclamation urging the people to obey the law. Nevertheless, the protest widened as people who worked hard for what little they had saw the law as oppressive. The federal government was aware of the continuing resistance but, for the

Whisky or *Whiskey?*

The traditional distinction is that *whiskey* is used for spirits from rebellious former British colonies and *whisky* for spirits from loyal former British colonies. Thus, Scotch and Canadian products are considered *whisky*, and Irish and American products are considered *whiskey*. The fact of the matter, however, is that spelling depends on brand. George Dickel uses *whisky*, while Jack Daniel's uses *whiskey*. Even within the same company there can be variation. Brown-Forman uses *whisky* for Old Forester and *whiskey* for Early Times.

moment, tried to settle the matter in the courts. And in some cases successful compromises were reached. For example, the collector of the federal tax in Kentucky was very sympathetic to the concerns of the distillers, as was the federal judge appointed to the state, and cases brought before his court usually resulted in taxes being collected only on the amount of whiskey actually produced, with generous terms of payment also being offered.

Although the Whiskey Rebellion was initially centered in western Pennsylvania, resistance to the tax spread throughout the frontier counties of Appalachia. In the spring of 1794, arrest warrants for people who refused to pay the tax began to be issued, armed militiamen joined the cause, and the protests turned violent.

Hamilton was not necessarily displeased with this turn of events. He and his supporters saw it as an opportunity to show the nation that the new federal government could and would enforce its laws, using force if necessary. Hamilton urged President Washington to raise an army and send it into western Pennsylvania to restore order. In August 1794, Washington issued another proclamation ordering the insurgents to disperse and also asked the governors of Pennsylvania, Maryland, New Jersey, and Virginia to provide fifteen thousand troops from their militias. He also sent three negotiators to western Pennsylvania to meet with David Bradford, the de facto leader of the insurgency, to attempt to find a peaceful resolution to the crisis. The negotiations failed, and the federal army left its encampment at Carlisle, Pennsylvania, on October 14 with Virginia governor Henry Lee at its head. Bradford and many of his supporters fled to Spanish Louisiana before the army arrived. The rest of the insurgents offered no resistance and were offered a chance to take an oath of allegiance to the United States. Many of those who refused were arrested, but only two people, Philip Wigle and John Mitchell, were actually convicted of treason. They were both pardoned by President Washington because he considered Mitchell to be a "simpleton" and Wigle "insane." The lack of prosecutions caused Thomas Jefferson to question Hamilton's motives in the whole affair, saying: "An insurrection was announced and proclaimed and armed against, but could never be found."[5] He would make the repeal of the whiskey tax part of his 1800 presidential campaign platform. After his election, he kept his promise by balancing the federal budget and, in 1802, repealing the whiskey tax, which was reimposed only when the government needed the money to pay for the War of 1812 and then the Civil War.

One of the legends to come out of the Whiskey Rebellion

was that the Kentucky distilling industry was created by those rebels fleeing Pennsylvania ahead of the federal troops. This was not the case. The distilling industry had been well established in Kentucky long before the rebellion. And the rebels, as we have seen, fled south, not west.

The whiskey tax did not do what Alexander Hamilton had hoped—force the development of larger distilleries with improved production capacities. Farm distilleries remained small-time business operations for many decades to come. Ironically, it is the licenses acquired during the whiskey tax days that give us our best view of these operations. Licenses indicate the number of stills involved, the capacity of each, the length of time distilling was authorized, and the licensee (not necessarily the owner). The license for a still owned by Daniel Weller, a farmer distiller and the grandfather of the distiller and rectifier William LaRue Weller, is a typical example. It indicates that Weller's neighbor, Jacob Hirsh, is authorized to use Weller's ninety-gallon still for the two weeks between September 18 and October 2, 1800.[6] Hirsh was therefore responsible for the taxes on the whiskey produced during that time period—probably about one hundred gallons.

Attempts were made to establish larger distilleries early in the nineteenth century. In 1816, for example, a group of investors from New England raised $100,000 and came to Louisville to build a modern distillery. They hoped that, by using European methods, they would produce a superior whiskey. The Hope Distillery, built in west Louisville at the foot of Sixteenth Street, housed two huge copper pot stills made from

Hope Distillery Grounds Becoming the Site of Louisville's First Horse Racetrack

The Hope Distillery was located at the foot of Sixteenth Street in West Louisville along the Ohio River. It closed only a few years after it opened in 1817, and the hundred-acre site was abandoned. In 1827, the Louisville Jockey Club announced that it would "commence the first Wednesday in October, 1827, on the Louisville turf, Hope Distillery, and continue four days. First day, three-mile heats, $120; second day, two-mile heats, $80; third day, one-mile heats, $50; fourth day, three best in five, one mile and repeat" (J. Stoddard Johnston, *Memorial History of Louisville from the First Settlement to the Year 1896* [New York: American Biographical Publishing Co., 1897], 323). The distillery site had become a horse racetrack.

a reported ten tons of copper and had the capacity to produce twelve hundred gallons of whiskey per day.[7] Like European distilleries, the Hope distilled its whiskey from a wort instead of a mash. A wort is made by cooking the grains into a sugary soup and removing the grain solids before fermenting the beer. A mash is fermented with the grain solids. Because the distillers were working with a wort, the corn was ground with the cob, the extra fiber working as a filter when the wort was drained from the mash. The idea was that distilling from a wort would prevent the grain from being scorched in the still and giving the whiskey a burned flavor, as was often the case with the whiskey made by the farmer distillers. But such large-scale production and such a high distillation proof also

License for Daniel Weller's distillery, 1800. This license is typical of the licenses issued during the years of the whiskey tax. (Courtesy Weller Family Papers, Filson Historical Society)

eliminated much of the grain flavor found in the farmer distiller–produced whiskey. The people of Kentucky still favored the whiskey produced in small pot stills, and the Hope Distillery failed by 1820. It would be several more decades before large-scale distilling would return to Louisville. In the meantime, the farmer distillers began making a new type of whiskey that they called *bourbon*.

2

The Origin of Bourbon Whiskey

What made bourbon famous was the aging process employed by its distillers, one that took place in charred oak barrels. It was known at least as early as the Roman Empire that water and wine stored in oak barrels charred on the inside stayed fresher longer. By the fifteenth century the process had been appropriated by the French to flavor and color brandy and cognac. And at some point in the early nineteenth century it was adopted by Kentucky distillers and allowed them to produce a whiskey with a sweet caramel/vanilla flavor and a red color.

Kentucky was a natural home for the manufacture of whiskey in that it has limestone-filtered water free of iron deposits, which can taint the flavor of whiskey. But it was especially suited to the manufacture of bourbon whiskey: its hot summers built up pressure in the barrels, allowing the fermenting liquid to enter the charred wood, and its cold winters reversed the process, allowing the whiskey to condense out of the wooden staves, bringing with it the caramelized sugars

Cognac and Charred Barrels

Cognac and other French brandies such as Armagnac are considered to be the first spirits to be aged in wood. Many wines are aged in toasted or charred barrels, so it is only natural that the early distillers of brandy made from wine would think of aging their product in wood.

contained in them. The state was also advantageously located in that the early distillers had easy access to the river systems that were key to the marketing of their product.

Beyond these general assertions, however, the origins and development of the early distilling industry in Kentucky and the bourbon industry in particular are mostly shrouded in mystery, and what little is known for certain is overshadowed by legend.

As far as distilling in general is concerned, one legend has it that the process was brought to Kentucky by settlers fleeing the Whiskey Rebellion. But, as we have seen, distilling in the state predates the unrest, not to mention the fact that those fleeing the rebellion would not have wished to linger in Kentucky, where they were subject to arrest by federal marshals. Another legend has it that it was specifically Scotch-Irish settlers who brought distilling with them, but a quick glance at the names of the early distilling families in the state—Myers, Calk, Williams, Pepper, Craig, Beam (Boehm), Weller, Spears, Ritchie, Davis—reveals the presence of a variety of cultures.

More specifically, Evan Williams has long been held to be Kentucky's first distiller, an assertion first made in 1892 by

Reuben Durrett, who claimed that as early as 1783 Williams's "whiskey had been distilled from corn."[1] This assertion does not, however, hold up under scrutiny. For one thing, the dating is disproved by the existence of a receipt for Williams's passage from London to Philadelphia on the ship *Pigoe* dated May 1, 1784.[2] More important, even if Williams had started distilling in 1783, there are other, more likely candidates for the honor of Kentucky's first distiller, among them Jacob Myers, who came to the state in 1779 and established a distillery on Dick's River, and the brothers Joseph and Samuel Davis, who arrived on horseback in 1779 bringing with them forty-gallon copper pot stills.[3]

The fact is that we may never know the identity of Kentucky's first distiller. For one thing, during the early days of the state's settlement, there was, as we have seen, no tax on distilled spirits and, thus, no government records on distillers. Also, many of the first settlers were barely literate, and the conditions under which all settlers lived would have been primitive, if not downright hostile, and, thus, unconducive to recordkeeping. The most likely source of evidence is the surviving personal letters, ledgers, and receipts of the distillers' customers. But to date nothing definitive has surfaced.

When it comes to the origin of bourbon whiskey, this too is an area where sources are hard to come by and legends again fill in the gaps. For a number of years, beginning in the late nineteenth century, the prime candidate for the title of the first distiller to create what is known today as bourbon whiskey was Elijah Craig, a Baptist minister and distiller in Scott County. In a history of Kentucky written more than sixty years after Craig's death in 1808, Richard Collins first indicated that Craig owned a fulling mill at Royal Spring (near Georgetown, Kentucky) and then, from the fact that the first bourbon was made in 1789 at a mill at Royal Spring, deduced that the distiller was Craig.[4] But no contemporary source tying Craig to the invention of bourbon whiskey has ever been found. And equally damning is a newspaper clipping from 1827, unearthed by Henry Crowgey, that reports a toast offered by the distiller Lewis Sanders at a dinner in Frankfort: "The memory of Elijah Craig, the founder of Georgetown, Kentucky. A philosopher and Christian—an useful man in his day. He established the first fulling mill, the first paper mill and the first rope walk in Kentucky. Honor to whom honor is done."[5] That the distillation of bourbon is not among the list of "firsts" offered in Craig's honor by a fellow distiller suggests that distilling was simply one of many enterprises in which Craig was engaged and certainly not the most noteworthy.

The name Elijah Craig also surfaces in discussions of the origins of the process by which bourbon is aged in which Craig is purported to have been the first person to have aged whiskey in charred barrels. One version of the story has him reusing barrels in which other products such as fish or nails had been shipped and charring their insides to remove any residue that would adversely affect the flavor of his whiskey. Another version has him making his own barrels and using materials that had been burned in a fire in the distillery cooperage. Both stories are implausible and easily dismissed, the first story on the grounds that barrels made to transport nails or fish would not have been watertight and, thus, would

Barrels

The barrel is often considered the medieval forklift. Barrels could be made to variable specifics in size, volume, and tightness, but their shape was always very similar. This shape allowed a barrel to be tipped on its side and rolled, but even a very heavy barrel could be controlled by a single person. Even after the invention in the nineteenth century of cardboard, which could be used for packaging, barrels were often used instead because of the ease of movement they afforded. Only with the invention of the forklift and pallets was the barrel superseded.

Whiskey thief and hydrometer kit. (Courtesy United Distillers Archive)

be unsuitable for the aging of whiskey, the second on the grounds that in an accidental fire staves would have burned on only one side and, thus, still have been suitable for barrel construction—not to mention the fact that a pillar of the community like Craig would hardly have been likely to risk his reputation and his livelihood by putting his whiskey in barrels made of charred wood had he not already been familiar with the process.

When and why bourbon whiskey came to be called *bourbon* is another mystery. Turning first to the question of when, the evidence is definitive of nothing save the fact that the name took a while to catch on. Searching through extant Kentucky newspapers from the first third of the nineteenth century, Crowgey found in a Bourbon County newspaper in 1821 "the first known advertisement featuring the distinctive Kentucky product," offered (by the barrel or the keg) by the Maysville firm of Stout and Adams under the name "BOURBON WHISKEY."[6] Nevertheless, when during his tour of the United States in 1824–1825—just a few years later—Lafayette visited Ashland, the home of Henry Clay, a Kentuckian offered a glass of "whiskey," not "bourbon whiskey" or "bourbon," to the health of the guest of honor. Had Kentucky bourbon achieved its reputation as high-quality whiskey, the record would have reflected that fact.[7]

Flash forward four decades, however, and the name seems to have been firmly established as that of a well-known style of whiskey. Another French dignitary visiting the United States, Prince Napoléon, was touring the camps at Staten Island in 1861 when he drank from a flask owned by one of the privates stationed there. He did not just enjoy the drink; he relished it. "What is it?" he asked. "Old Bourbon, Sir," replied the soldier. "Old Bourbon indeed," was the prince's response. "I did not think I would like anything with that name so well."[8]

Turning to why bourbon came to be called *bourbon,* legends, again, abound. One of the oldest is that the name comes from Bourbon County, Kentucky. Supposedly, merchants in New Orleans found that shipments of whiskey carrying invoices indicating that they came from "Limestone, Bourbon County, Kentucky," were the most desirable. Their customers soon started asking for that "Bourbon County" whiskey, and the reference was eventually shortened to simply *bourbon whiskey.* There are two problems with this legend. The first is that in these early years of settlement there was limited trade with New Orleans (the round trip took a year) and that it is therefore unlikely that there were enough whiskey shipments invoiced to Limestone to catch the attention of New Orleanians. The second is that Limestone (the present-day Maysville) was part of Bourbon County for only a very brief time while Kentucky was still part of Virginia and that by the time bourbon became a style of whiskey being advertised in Kentucky newspapers the town had been a part of Mason County for more than three decades. The oral tradition connecting the name to Bourbon County is strong, however. If there is any truth to it, most likely the bourbon–Bourbon County connection was made for pure marketing reasons after the 1803 Louisiana Purchase. It is also possible that the name came from river travelers drinking the aged whiskey of New Orleans on Bourbon Street and starting to ask for that "Bourbon Street whiskey."

It is unlikely that the origins of bourbon whiskey will ever be known for certain, but a theory can be formed on the basis of the available evidence. For one thing, bourbon whiskey is aged whiskey, and, as bourbon ages, it decreases in volume owing to both evaporation and absorption into the wood. Since the whiskey tax called for payment as soon as the whiskey was barreled, while the tax was still in force it seems unlikely that, after paying the tax, a distiller would have held on to the whiskey, aged it, and thus suffered a loss. This then places the origin of bourbon no earlier than 1802, when the tax was repealed, and, given that the tax was reinstated in 1814, possibly as late as 1817, when the tax was again repealed.

It should be noted as well that there seems to have been very little profit to be made from the sale of unaged whiskey. For example, we know from records kept by the Bourbon County distiller John Corlis in the early 1820s that the price for whiskey in New Orleans was "40@43," or forty gallons at $43, very close to the cost of whiskey in Kentucky.[9] When the whiskey tax was repealed in 1817, therefore, there would have been a great incentive to age the spirit, making it more attractive to consumers and, thus, more profitable.

It can further be inferred that it was probably not a distiller who invented bourbon whiskey but more likely a grocer or a wholesale whiskey merchant, someone who saw that the people of New Orleans were not buying unaged corn whiskey, preferring instead brandy and cognac imported from France,

John Corlis and His Gin Distillery

John Corlis made gin in Providence, Rhode Island, and wrote several letters during the War of 1812 complaining about the coastal embargo keeping him from getting rye for his distillery. He writes in one letter that he complained to a government official that he could not pay his distillery taxes if he could not get the rye he needed (letter of March 1814, Corlis-Respess Family Papers, Filson Historical Society, Louisville). In another he wrote that the "embargo on the coastal trade . . . does indeed look to me more of a hostility to New England than old England" (letter of January 4, 1814, Corlis-Respess Family Papers).

products that had been aged in charred barrels. Tellingly, the earliest reference to charring barrels to be found so far comes from a July 15, 1826, letter from a Lexington grocer to John Corlis. The grocer had purchased barrels of whiskey from Corlis before and was writing to obtain more. After indicating that he would like to receive eight to ten barrels per week, he added: "It is suggested to me that if the barrels should be burnt upon the inside, say only a 16th of an inch, that it will much improve it, of this however I presume you are the best judge."[10]

As for the name, it is likely that *bourbon* was chosen to make the product more marketable. Whether the reference was to the French royal family or to Bourbon County, Kentucky, which had been named after the royal family, the appeal would have been to sentiment, particularly among the large French population in New Orleans.

If the foregoing speculation is correct, there is a likely

Toasted or Charred?

The difference between toasting a barrel and charring a barrel is that between heating and burning. When a barrel is toasted, heat is applied to the wood, but the wood is not allowed to catch on fire and burn. The intense heat works to soften the wood fibers, allowing the staves to be bent into the traditional barrel shape. The heat also starts to break down the cellulose in the wood and creates vanilla flavors in it. Charring occurs when the cooper allows the inside of the barrel to catch fire and burn. The longer the wood burns, the deeper the layer of char on the inside of the barrel. Charring the wood creates a "red layer" of natural, caramelized sugars. This layer adds the caramel flavors to bourbon, while the toasted wood adds the vanilla flavors.

candidate for the creator of bourbon—or, rather, two candidates, the Tarascon brothers, Louis and John. They were born in Cabannes, France, not far from the Cognac region. Louis fled the Reign of Terror and came to Philadelphia in 1789. John followed in 1797 to join his brother in business. They moved to Pittsburgh and started a shipyard, with the goal of building vessels capable of both river and ocean travel, but, after losing a ship over the Falls of the Ohio in 1803, it was clear to them that their shipyard needed to be located below that natural obstacle. While they never did build this new shipyard, by 1807 they had established a small mill at Shippingport, Kentucky, and they also built a warehouse at the falls. From there they established trade with New Orleans and were in the perfect position to purchase whiskey coming down the river, age it, ship the better-tasting product to New Orleans, and sell it.

Whatever its origins, bourbon gave Kentucky a reputation for making fine whiskey. That reputation grew with the new nation and spread across the United States as the Industrial Revolution facilitated travel and improved communications.

3

The Industrial Revolution and the Distilling Industry

The Industrial Revolution transformed the distilling industry in America. What was a cottage industry at the beginning of the nineteenth century had developed into a fully fledged factory system by the century's end.

Driving the Industrial Revolution was the steam engine. Steam power facilitated manufacturing processes, allowing for the mass production of goods and improvements in transportation. Cities became centers of production, and rural populations declined as people abandoned the countryside for urban areas.

The first practical application of steam power to transportation was the steamboat. By 1787 the inventor John Fitch was operating steamboats on the Delaware River, but the venture failed through lack of funding, and it was not until 1807 that Robert Fulton and his financial backer, Robert Livingston, developed the first commercial steamboat, which carried passengers between New York City and Albany, New York.

John Fitch

John Fitch was not a well-educated gentleman from the upper crust of society. Unable to secure the funding to realize his patented steamboat design in the East—purportedly because of his plain talk and common manner—he moved west, settling in Bardstown, Kentucky, in the 1790s. His hope that the ordinary people of the West would have greater vision than eastern politicians and bankers was, however, never realized. He fell into a depression that led to the drinking and opium use that ultimately killed him.

The new technology soon moved west. The steamboat *New Orleans* was launched in Pittsburgh in 1811 and sailed downriver to New Orleans, thereafter plying the waters between New Orleans and Natchez until it sank in 1814. In 1815, the steamboat *Enterprise* made the first round-trip from Pittsburgh to New Orleans. Within five years there were sixty-nine steamboats sailing western rivers.

The increase in river traffic spurred the development of canal systems, which improved river travel by bypassing river hazards as well as linking major waterways, allowing goods to be shipped farther and faster. But their hegemony was short-lived. The American railway mania, which began in the late 1820s with the development of the steam locomotive, sent the Industrial Revolution into overdrive.

The first common carrier, the Baltimore and Ohio Railroad, was chartered in 1827 and started operations in 1830. Chartered in the same year, the South Carolina Railroad start-

Flatboats and Shotgun Houses

When merchants from Kentucky sailed their flatboats down to New Orleans, part of the profit from the trip came from selling the flatboats at the end of the journey. While flatboats had no value as boats in New Orleans—they were not seaworthy, and they could not travel back upstream—they had value as sources of lumber. They were broken down, and the lumber thereby salvaged was used to build houses. It is said that many of the oldest shotgun-style houses found in New Orleans are built from lumber salvaged from flatboats.

ed its operations in 1833. Despite their initial limited reach, both quickly became profitable enterprises, and they, and the industry as a whole, continued to grow. Almost three thousand miles of track had been laid by 1840, a figure that had grown to over thirty thousand miles by 1860. Passengers and freight were being moved across the nation as far west as St. Joseph, Missouri.

Cities that found themselves developing as shipping and railroad hubs prospered the most from the Industrial Revolution. One such city was Louisville, Kentucky. It was perfectly positioned to become a center of river trade, situated as it was just below the Falls of the Ohio, the only natural obstruction on the Ohio River and passable only when river levels were exceptionally high. The desirability of a canal to the city's shipping interests was recognized as early as 1781, but all attempts to mount a state-funded project failed. Finally, the Louisville and Portland Canal Company—a private venture—was char-

Louisville and Portland Canal

Even though the invention of the railroad made longer canal projects such as the Erie Canal obsolete, the smaller canals around river hazards such as the Louisville and Portland Canal, which bypassed the Falls of the Ohio, remained very practical. In 1855, the federal government, which had become the majority stockholder of the Louisville and Portland, placed the canal under the control of the Army Corps of Engineers. By 1874, the government had become the sole owner of the canal. The Louisville and Portland Canal has been improved and widened several times since it opened. It remains a valuable part of the Ohio River traffic even in the twenty-first century.

tered by the state legislature in 1825, and, in December 1830, the *Uncas* became the first steamboat to pass through the locks of the canal. The Ohio River had become navigable both upstream and down.

The railroad came to the city in 1847 with the construction of the Louisville and Frankfort Railroad. The Louisville and Nashville Railroad Company was formed in 1849–1850. The line to Nashville was completed in 1859, and two lines making the connection to Memphis opened in 1861. By the end of the Civil War (1861–1865), Louisville was established as a center for railroad traffic. Once the first transcontinental railroad was completed—in 1869—and railroad bridges over the Ohio opened—the Fourteenth Street Bridge in 1870 and the Kentucky and Indiana Bridge in 1886—the city was

Aerial view of Bonnie Bros. Distillery, Louisville, with a railroad round-house in the background, ca. 1940. (Courtesy United Distillers Archive)

connected with northern and western as well as southern markets.

It was inevitable, then, that Louisville would become the marketing center of the Kentucky bourbon industry. Whiskey Row eventually stretched for over a dozen blocks on Water, Main, and Market Streets between Preston Street on the east and Tenth Street on the west, populated by the sales offices of distillers, wholesale companies, and rectifiers from around the state. But the changes wrought by the Industrial Revolution also facilitated the building of larger-scale distilleries in urban areas—previously an impossibility. Corn, rye, and malted barley could be shipped in, whether by steamboat or train, and steam-powered pumps allowed the distilleries to drill deep wells for a constant source of cool water. (Distilleries were still built in rural areas, of course, but they had to be close to a railroad line to ensure an adequate supply line and a connection to the markets.) So it was inevitable that Louisville would become a distilling center of the Kentucky bourbon industry as well.

Distilleries also developed technologically over the course of the nineteenth century. The earliest application of steam power to the distilling process was, as we have seen, the 1816–1820 Hope Distillery experiment. But it was only with the invention of the column still some ten years later that steam power came to be the major source of heat for distilleries.

In 1831, the Irish inventor Aeneas Coffey patented the column, or continuous, still. The column still differed from a pot still in that it was fed by a continuous flow of distiller's beer (the fermented mash of grains), allowing for large quantities of alcohol to be made in a single run. It is a large apparatus, often as much as three to five feet in diameter and two to three stories tall, segmented approximately every three feet by plates perforated with many small holes and one large hole. Beer is fed into the upper part of the still, covering the plates, and flowing down the segments through the larger holes, which are offset so that the beer flows in a zigzag pattern. Steam pumped into the bottom of the still rises up through the small holes in the plates to the top of the still. As it rises, it strips the alcohol from the beer. The alcohol-laden steam is removed near the top and condensed in a worm, producing the distilled spirit. The spent beer is removed from the bottom of the still, some of it being reused as backset or souring for the sour mash process, and the rest being sold as cattle feed, either in liquid form or dried.

The big advantage of the column still was that it produced a large amount of alcohol cheaply. With pot stills, the solids had to be removed from the mash before distilling, and the still had to be cleaned after each batch. With column stills, the solids could remain in the mash. The rising steam kept the solids from drying and scorching and, thus, adding a burned flavor to the whiskey. As long as beer was continuously fed into the still, alcohol could be produced. The column still also allowed the production of alcohol that was higher proof—as high 95 percent—and contained little or no grain oil and, thus, was flavorless. This high-proof alcohol would be an important factor in the business of rectifying whiskey.

Column stills took large amounts of beer to run at full capacity, requiring larger vats or tubs for fermenting the mash to make the beer. Larger fermenting vats, in turn, increased

Proof

Proof is simply the percentage of alcohol by volume, doubled—one hundred proof is 50 percent alcohol by volume (ABV). The term *proof* comes from the times when distillers would "prove" their product by gunpowder. They would mix their spirit with gunpowder and set it on fire. If it sputtered and smoked, it was determined that it was "under proof." If it burned too quickly with a high flame, it was "over proof." If it burned with a steady flame, then it was "100 percent proved." This even burn happens when the alcohol content of the whiskey is 50 percent ABV.

The column still at Buffalo Springs Distillery, Stamping Grounds, Kentucky, ca. 1943. (Courtesy United Distillers Archive)

the demand for grain, a demand that could grow so great that grain often had to be shipped in from out of state. This grain was most likely ground at the distillery using a steam mill, either a roller mill or a hammer mill. A roller mill is simply a steam-powered version of the old water mill with a mill stone to produce the meal. A hammer mill uses metal hammers to pound the grain into meal.

Other innovations followed as well. In 1869, Marshall J. Allen, of the firm Paris, Allen and Company, the New York distributors of Old Crow for the firm Gaines, Berry and Company, patented coiled metal heating and cooling tubes for mash tubs.[1] Regulating the temperature of the mash is an essential part of the brewing process. For starters, yeast dies when the mash gets too hot; it also lives longer when the heat is kept down, permitting the production of more alcohol. Furthermore, the different grains that make up the mash cook at different temperatures: corn at the highest, followed by rye or wheat and then barley malt. The coils facilitated the necessary temperature regulation. They also allowed for an expanded distilling season, which had traditionally been confined largely to the winter months.

The warehouses in which whiskey was aged also saw technological innovations. Through the 1870s, whiskey barrels were stored in Kentucky in the same manner they were stored in Europe: lined up in rows stacked three and four high and separated by wooden rails resting on the barrel tops. There are several problems with this storage method. The weight of the stack can cause leaks in the barrels in the bottom rows. There is little room for air to circulate, promoting the growth of mold and, thus, musty-tasting whiskey. Finally, removing barrels from the middle of the bottom row was extremely labor intensive, involving as it did moving and then replacing all the barrels in the upper rows.

All that changed when, in 1879, Frederick Stitzel patented a system of tiered storage racks.[2] Each warehouse floor housed three tiers of barrels. The first tier was stored on four-inch-square wooden rails positioned at ground level, and the second and third tiers were stored on rails positioned just above the tops of the first and second levels of barrels. This method allowed for easier access to the barrels (upper-level barrels did not need to be moved when removing lower-level barrels), eliminated the pressure placed on the lower levels by the upper levels, and increased the circulation of air around the barrels.

The process by which whiskey was aged also saw im-

Patent model for barrel rack by Frederick Stitzel, 1879. (Courtesy Filson Historical Society)

provements. Recognizing that most aging occurred during the summer months, when the warm temperatures caused the liquid to expand into the wood, distillers began building warehouses that could be heated in the winter months to speed up the process. A less successful attempt involved inserting a metal heating element directly into the whiskey barrel via the bunghole.[3] This patented method never caught on, however, partly because it was not practical on a large scale, and partly because it tended to spark fires in the barrels.

Distilleries saw improvements other than the technological during the course of the nineteenth century. Dr. James Crow, for example, who was trained in medicine and chemistry in his native Scotland, brought the use of scientific method with him when he emigrated to Kentucky in the 1820s and

Bourbon labels from an 1850 scrapbook of a Louisville printer named Miller. (Courtesy Filson Historical Society)

went to work at the Old Oscar Pepper Distillery in Woodford County (with which he stayed for all but two years of his career, 1837–1838, when he worked for Newton Henry's distillery). His object was to learn more about what went on in each step of the process, about what worked and what did not, and then keep a careful record of his results so that a more consistent and better product could be achieved.

In theory, the distilling process is quite simple: two things go into the still, beer and steam, and two things come out, alcohol and spent mash. In reality, however, as Crow recognized, there are many variables in the process that make distilling a real art. For example, the temperature at which the alcohol is removed determines the proof of the final product, but it also determines the congeners left behind, congeners being the by-products of the yeast and grain in the beer that flavor the alcohol.

Among his innovations, Crow used a thermometer to record temperature, a hydrometer to check alcohol levels, and litmus paper to check the pH at each step of the whiskey-making process. Using these and other means he attained an understanding of what made good whiskey good and bad whiskey bad. He is also credited with realizing the importance of limestone water in making bourbon whiskey, with improving the sour mash process, with improving sanitation around the distillery (moving the hog lots and cattle pens—a side business that took advantage of the spent beer—to a safe distance), even with being the father of modern bourbon.

The Old Oscar Pepper Distillery was in Crow's day never a huge operation. It produced only about three barrels of

A steamboat loading barrels from the Darling Distillery near Carrolton, Kentucky, ca. 1880. (Courtesy United Distillers Archive)

bourbon a day and, because at that time distilling remained confined to the winter months, likely no more than one thousand barrels a year. Even so, Crow's whiskey, which went by the name Crow or Old Crow—gained a national reputation for its quality and was favored by the likes of Kentucky senator Henry Clay.

Crow died in 1856 and was succeeded at the distillery by William F. Mitchell.[4] Crow left no heir, and Oscar Pepper eventually sold what remained of Crow's whiskey, along with the rights to the brand name Old Crow, to W. A. Gaines. In 1868, Gaines formed Gaines, Berry and Company, a firm that also included E. H. Taylor Jr., and Taylor spent the next year traveling Europe and examining the design of distilleries in

Scotland, Ireland, England, Italy, France, and Germany, looking for the best and most modern methods to bring home with him. On his return, Gaines, Berry and Company used what Taylor had learned to build a new distillery to make Old Crow bourbon. The firm hired William F. Mitchell away from the Old Oscar Pepper Distillery, and he brought with him Crow's notebooks for reference, thus guaranteeing that Old Crow remained a high-quality product, the standard against which other bourbons would be judged in the years to come.

All these innovations changed the face of the bourbon industry in Kentucky. It was becoming a big business and an expensive one at that—far beyond the reach of the typical farmer distiller, for whom distilling was only a side business. The farmer distiller did not, however, die off immediately, and there remained people who preferred their whiskey made the old-fashioned way. This small but steady market led, as we will see in the next chapter, to the rise of the rectifiers and a marketing revolution born out of the competition between the rectifiers and the straight whiskey distillers.

4

Distillers and Rectifiers

As the reputation of Kentucky bourbon grew, so did the number of people who wanted to take advantage of that reputation by marketing a cheap imitation. These people were wholesale merchants—also known as *rectifiers*—who would purchase cheap whiskey, "rectify" (i.e., purify and/or flavor) it, and then resell it. (Louisville's Whiskey Row was, during the first half of the nineteenth century, populated mostly by such wholesale merchants.) Initially, the rectifiers were supplied by farmer distillers with unaged white spirits of various proofs that had to be redistilled and filtered through charcoal to remove unwanted flavors and reflavored by aging in charred barrels. As the century progressed, the invention of the column still gave them an added source of whiskey that was both cheap and distilled to a very high proof, making it neutral in taste. Flavoring and coloring methods were also developed that allowed them to bypass the aging process. They rarely came close to matching the taste of a true bourbon, but the end result was cheap and sweet and, thus, easy to market. It also took only hours, and not four years, to produce.

Rectifiers' Flavoring and Coloring Agents

Rectifiers used many different products to make their whiskey. "Burnt sugar" is brown sugar used to sweeten and color the alcohol. Prune juice and cherry juice were also used to color and flavor the alcohol. Some of the more unusual products include creosote and cochineal. Creosote is the oily product used to preserve the wood of utility poles. Cochineal is a red dye made from the crushed, dried bodies of the female cochineal insect (*Dactylopius coccus*), which lives on cacti of Central America and Mexico.

Not surprisingly, recipes for these imitation products were in great demand. One example of the books that began to appear on the market in response is Pierre Lacour's ca. 1860 *The Manufacture of Liquors, Wines and Cordials without the Aid of Distillation.* Lacour gives recipes for rectified or imitation Irish, Scotch, and American styles of whiskey as well as many different styles of brandy and cordials. These products all use neutral spirits as a primary ingredient, and most do not use any aged whiskey at all. Examples of Lacour's recipes for whiskey include the following:

Irish Whiskey: Neutral spirits, four gallons; refined sugar, three pounds, in water, four quarts; creosote, four drops; color with four ounces burnt sugar.

Scotch Whiskey: Neutral spirits, four gallons; alcoholic solution of starch, one gallon; creosote, five drops; cochineal tincture, four wine glasses full; burnt sugar coloring, quarter of a pint.

Oronoko Rye Whiskey: Neutral Spirit, four gallons; refined sugar, three and a half pounds; water, to dissolve, three pints; decoction of tea, one pint; burnt sugar, four ounces, oil of pear, half an ounce; dissolved in an ounce of alcohol.

Tuscaloosa Whiskey: Neutral spirits, four pints; honey, three pints; dissolved in water, four pints; solution of starch, five pints; oil of wintergreen, four drops, dissolved in half an ounce of acetic ether; color with four ounces burnt sugar.

Old Bourbon Whiskey: Neutral spirits, four gallons; refined sugar, three pounds, dissolved in water, three quarts; decoction of tea, one pint; three drops of oil of wintergreen, dissolved in one ounce of alcohol; color with tincture of cochineal, two ounces; burnt sugar, three ounces.

Monongahela Whiskey: Neutral spirit, four gallons; honey, three pints, dissolved in water, one gallon; rum, half gallon; nitric ether, half an ounce. This is to be colored to suit fancy. Some customers prefer this whiskey transparent, while others like it just perceptibly tinged with brown; while others, again, want it rather deep, and partaking of red.[1]

These recipes are valuable for two reasons. First and foremost, they offer direct evidence of the way in which cheap whiskey was being produced. But they also offer indirect evidence about the products that were being imitated. For example, in 1853, when *The Manufacture of Liquors* was published, Monongahela whiskey was not always aged. We know this because the recipe for Lacour's version indicates that the color should depend on customer preference and that unaged/ uncolored, slightly aged/lightly colored, and more extensively aged/deeply colored versions were all available on the market. Bourbon, on the other hand, should always have a deep red color (imparted by cochineal) and tannic and minty flavors (imparted by tea and wintergreen, respectively). American whiskeys were evidently sweet—sugar is Lacour's prime ingredient—with Monongahela and Tuscaloosa whiskeys in particular being known for their strong honey flavor. Scotch whiskey should be deeply colored but not sweet (the only flavoring ingredients are starch and creosote). Irish whiskey seems to have been midway between Scotch and American whiskeys since the recipe calls for some sugar but also for some creosote.

The nineteenth century was not all smooth sailing for the distilling industry. The Civil War proved a disruption to business. This was especially true in the South, where spirits were prohibited (they could be used only by the Confederate army for medicinal purposes) and copper stills were confiscated and melted down for the manufacture of war materiel. The main effects in the North were the imposition of a federal tax on the production of distilled spirits to pay for the war[2] and the creation of a lawless atmosphere in some border states, especially Kentucky and Tennessee. (Charles D. Weller and Mc-Wiley Parker of the Louisville whiskey firm W. L. Weller and Bro. were robbed and murdered by two gunmen in Clarksville, Tennessee, in July 1862 while traveling on business.)[3] Still, the demand for whiskey remained strong in both the Union and the Confederacy, and Kentucky distilleries were more than ready to fulfill it.

The strength of the Kentucky distilling industry is evident in the listings under *whiskey* in the 1864–1865 edition of Edwards's annual directory for the city of Louisville:

Anthony Jacobs & Co. 133 4th between Main and Water. Bartlett, V. R. & Sons 62 Main between 6th & 7th. Billing and Druesbach 310 Main between 3rd & 4th. Block, H. & Co. 833 Main between 8th & 9th. Boes, John & Co. 119 Market between 1st & 2nd. Clark, James A. & Co. 219 3rd between Main and Market. Clarke, Samuel S. 119 Market between 1st & 2nd. Clary, Francis Main between 11th & 12th. Cochran, John & Son 330 Main between 3rd & 4th. Cowan, D. H. 724 Main between 7th & 8th. Cropper, Patton & Co. 143 & 145 4th between Main and Water. Crump, Ropert H. 208 Main. Dorn, Barkhouse & Co. 428 Main between Bullitt and 5th. Finck, C. Henry 310 Market between 3rd & 4th. Gaetano, V. D. & Co. 700 Main between 7th & 8th. Gheens, John R. & Bro. 308 Main between 3rd & 4th. Koch & Leonhard 201 Market between 2nd & 3rd. Lanham, James T. 3rd between Market and Jefferson. Laval, Jacob 120 & 122 2nd between Main and Water. Lichten, A. & Bro. 219 5th between Main and Market. McDermott, James & Co. 716 Main between 7th & 8th. Monks, J. & Co. 732 Main between 7th & 8th. Moore, Bremaker & Co. 722 Main between 7th & 8th. Nuttall, R. & Sons 236 Market between 2nd & 3rd. Ratel, William 135 4th between Main and Water. Schaeffer, F. J. Market between 6th & 7th. Schrodt & Woebler 5th between Main and Water. Schroeder, J. H. & Sons 28 Wall. Shrader, R. A. & Co. 210

E. Market above Brook. Smith, A. T. & R. L. 2nd between Main and Water. Somerville, C. H. 620 Market between 6th and 7th. Stege, Reiling & Co. 232 Market between 2nd & 3rd. Taylor, E. H. Main se corner 7th. Terfloth, John C. & Co. 138 4th near Main. Thierman, H. & Co. 614 Market between 6th and 7th. Thompson & Co. 79 4th between Main and Market. Vissing, Herman Jefferson between Jackson and Hancock. Walker, W. H. & Co. 206 Main. Welby, George 336 Main between 3rd and 4th. Weller & Buckner 612 Main between 6th and 7th. Wolf, Charles and Co. Main between 11th and 12th. Zahone, A. & Sons 145 5th between Main and Water.[4]

No companies on this list survive today, but there are a few familiar names. We find, for instance, William LaRue Weller, who partnered with a man named Buckner after his brother Charles was murdered. And we also find E. H. Taylor, whom we met in the previous chapter.

Taylor is an important figure in the postwar distilling industry in that he was one of the earliest to grasp the concept of marketing and was very skilled at promoting his products and creating brand recognition. One of his first efforts at promotion involved Old Crow after Gaines, Berry and Company had assumed production. It came to his attention that, while a guest at the home of General Benjamin Butler in Washington, DC, Judge George Washington Woodward of Pennsylvania was bragging about the quality of a twenty-year-old rye whiskey from Pennsylvania, claiming that it was as good as any Kentucky bourbon. William Brown of Kentucky, who was present at the time, took up the challenge and wrote to the

E. H. Taylor Jr.

Edmund Haynes Taylor was born at Columbus, Kentucky, in the Jackson Purchase region of western Kentucky in 1830. His grandfather, Richard Taylor Jr., was the surveyor for the state, and his father, John Taylor, traded merchandise and slaves between Kentucky and New Orleans. Edmund was only five years old when his father died of disease—probably typhus—while returning to Kentucky from New Orleans. Edmund lived with his great-uncle Zachary Taylor for a while before going to Lexington to live with his Uncle Edmund Haynes Taylor, who saw to it that he was well educated. It in this period that he added the *Jr.* to his name.

Thanks to his uncle's connections, E. H. Taylor Jr. entered the banking business in 1854 as a partner in the firm Taylor, Turner and Co. This firm became Taylor, Shelby and Co. in the year 1855, and it catered to many of the important people in Lexington, from Cassius Clay to John Hunt Morgan. The bank failed in the financial troubles of 1857, and Taylor went into the commodities business. During his travels with the bank and as a commodities trader, he saw a Lincoln-Douglas debate and stayed at a boarding house in Missouri with William Tecumseh Sherman. During the Civil War, he traded in cotton after using his connections with John J. Crittenden to secure permission to acquire cotton in Memphis, Tennessee. He also entered into the liquor trade with an office on Whiskey Row in Louisville in 1864.

Taylor toured European distilleries in 1866, learning the latest in distilling technology and technique. He returned to the United States and applied this knowledge to the design of the Hermitage Distillery. In 1869, he purchased the Swigert Distillery, on the banks of the Kentucky River in Leestown. He rebuilt it—renaming it the OFC (or Old-Fashioned Copper) Distillery—using the knowledge he gained in Europe. He was determined to make it not only a great distillery but also an attractive distillery that could be shown with pride to potential customers. He paid attention to the small details. This was a pot still distillery that made "old-fashioned copper" bourbon in the tradition of James C. Crow. The buildings were of brick and steel with modern "patent" warehouses with barrel ricks and steam heat. Taylor also paid attention to the package the bourbon he sold came in—the barrel. He insisted on brass rings for the barrels and made sure they were all clean and bright before being shipped to a customer. He promoted his whiskey by publicizing letters of recommendation from important customers, prints of the distillery for display, and all the other advertising paraphernalia offered at the time. He was his own marketing department and advertising agency before most people had ever heard of such things.

Taylor would fall victim to bad financial times and an overproduction of whiskey, losing control of the distillery in 1878 to the firm Gregory and Stagg from St. Louis. He eventually created the bourbon brand Old Taylor and rebuilt another distillery to make it. He championed the Bottled-in-Bond Act of 1897 and the Pure Food and Drug Act of 1906. He became the mayor of Frankfort and a leader in the movement that kept the capital in Frankfort when the state decided it needed a larger statehouse to house the government.

When Prohibition took effect in 1920, Taylor tried to fight it in the courts but failed. He was out of the whiskey business. In his forced retirement, he concentrated on breeding Hereford cattle. He died in Frankfort on January 19, 1923, just weeks short of his eighty-third birthday.

firm Paris and Allen, the distributor of Old Crow in New York City, asking for a bourbon aged at least fifteen years so that it could be compared to Woodward's preferred brand. Paris and Allen in turn contacted Taylor, who sent Brown a bottle of twenty-year-old Old Crow to represent Kentucky bourbon in the ensuing contest of honor. After the contest, Taylor issued the following press release:

Important decision at Washington!! Kentucky vs. Pennsylvania. Old Bourbon vs. Old Rye. A decision has just been rendered at Washington which cannot fail to be of particular interest to our readers. We give a sketch of the case as related to us. "An evening not long since at Genl. Butler's residence in Washington, Judge Woodward of Pennsylvania remarked that he knew of some Rye Whiskey over 20 years old that was made in his state which would excel any Bourbon ever distilled. The gauntlet thus thrown down was instantly accepted by the Hon. Wm. Brown of Kentucky. He wrote at once to Mssrs. W. A. Gaines & Co., Frankfort, Ky.—(owners of the celebrated Hermitage Distillery) for a bottle of the finest 'Bourbon' Kentucky could produce, while Judge Woodward procured a bottle of the 'Rye.' Mssrs. Gaines & Co. after a careful comparison selected a bottle of the renowned 'Old Crow' (of which they are also proprietors) made by the old Scotchman himself 21 years ago. As both samples were over 21 years of age, they were fully mature, and though not able to vote were fitting representatives of their respective States. The Court being duly convened with that eminent connoisseur, Genl. Butler as presiding judge, the case was called. Both sides being ready, counsel at once proceeded upon the merits and while ably argued, the samples themselves were more spiritually eloquent. After the evidence was all in and well digested, the judgement was rendered in favor of Kentucky's 'Old Crow' as being the most mellow, rich, full yet delicately flavored and surpassing in boquet." We congratulate Mssrs. W. A. Gaines & Co. on their success, which they richly deserve, as they have devoted years of study to the perfection of distillation and spared no expense in pursuit of purity and quality. The "Hermitage" Distillery, of which Frankfort is justly proud, is a result of their labors, and its product though not two years old has an unequaled reputation both at home and abroad.[5]

What Taylor was doing was "branding" Old Crow. That is, he was bringing it to national attention in a context that reinforced the quality and, presumably, the reliability of his product and, thus, creating a demand for it among consumers who until that point preferred familiar, locally produced whiskey. He was also piggybacking on the reputation of the Old Oscar Pepper Distillery, the original maker of Old Crow, to brand the newly formed Gaines, Berry and Company. He would similarly market his own future distilling ventures.

Taylor was not alone in grasping the importance of branding. Others followed his lead, giving birth to a marketing revolution that swept the distilling industry. Equally important to the marketing revolution were Hiram Walker and the Brown brothers.

Hiram Walker was born in the United States but built a distillery in Ontario, Canada, in 1858 and started producing what he called Walker's Club whiskey. He decided not to sell his whiskey until it was properly aged and then, to ensure

Old Dixie advertising painting, ca. 1895. (Courtesy Filson Historical Society)

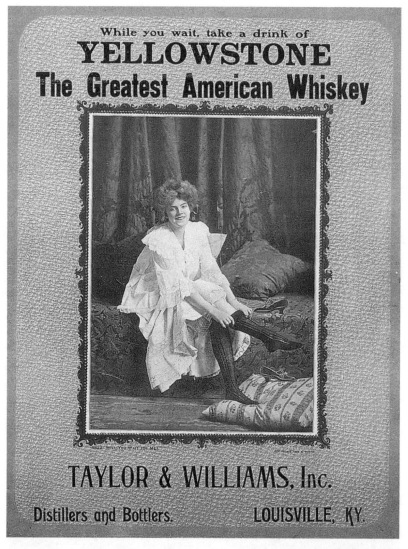

Yellowstone advertisement, ca. 1890. (Courtesy United Distillers Archive)

quality, to sell it only by the bottle. Walker's Club became very popular when it was released to the market in the 1860s, and soon there were hundreds of whiskeys calling themselves *club* whiskeys. In 1873, Congress passed legislation requiring that the country of origin be stated on all imported whiskeys, and Walker's Club became Canadian Club.

The success of Canadian Club caused Hiram Walker to spend a lot of time in court defending his brand from imitators and frauds. It was apparent that the industry needed a way to register brand names, and soon the companies were publishing claims to their brands in the major trade magazines such as *Mida's Criteria* in Chicago and *Bonfort's Wine and Spirits* in New York. These claims were later used as proof of ownership when the U.S. government passed its first trademark registration rules in 1881. The industry continued to publish trademarks in the trade magazines up until Prohibition.

In the United States, George Garvin Brown and his brother J. T. S. Brown Jr. created a whiskey firm and, with it, the brand Old Forester in the year 1870. The firm would change names several times before the end of the century, eventually becoming Brown-Forman (as it is known today), but George Garvin Brown stayed on as its head, and Old Forester remained his main brand of bourbon whiskey. Like Walker, the Browns too decided to sell their whiskey only by the bottle. Their rationale was somewhat different, however. Whiskey was a popular medicine at the time, but physicians resisted prescribing it because it was sold mostly by the barrel and quality could vary greatly from barrel to barrel. Old Forester was the first bourbon to be available exclusively in bottles—sealed bottles that assured a greater level of quality assurance. The Browns named their whiskey for the Louisville physician William Forrester (the second *r* was dropped from the name after Forrester retired). They then designed a label that looks very much like

George Garvin Brown with an
Old Forester bottle. (Courtesy
Brown-Forman Distillery)

a physician's prescription and includes a handwritten claim to
quality: "Nothing Better in the Market."

As brand names grew, so did their marketing ventures.
Advertisements (by now in color) in newspapers and magazines
were employed to make brand names known to consumers.
Jugs and decanters, glassware and swizzle sticks, emblazoned
with the brand name were manufactured and sold to consumers very cheaply. Similarly adorned mirrors and artwork could
be purchased from the distilleries for display in bars and saloons. Booklets describing distilleries and brands were published. The marketing revolution was in full swing.

The distillers and rectifiers quickly learned that, the more
they promoted their brand, the more they sold. But they also
learned that they had to be on their guard against trademark
infringement and counterfeiting. One distiller, James E. Pepper, attempted to thwart counterfeiters by affixing strip stamps
carrying his signature across the corks in his bottles of whiskey. His advertisements warned consumers to buy only bottles

Mammoth Cave bar decanters, ca. 1890. (Courtesy United Distillers Archive)

Whiskey jug. (Courtesy United Distillers Archive)

with intact stamps. Otherwise, they may not be buying "Genuine Pepper" whiskey. The concept of the strip stamp over the cork would later be taken up by the government in the form of tax stamps.

By the end of the nineteenth century Kentucky's whiskey industry had earned a national reputation for producing a quality product. This product was well advertised and was available in all states of the Union as well as markets abroad. With this success came increased profits—and greater incentive to imitate the product. This state of affairs would divide the industry and create the need for legislation laying out guidelines for what could be considered whiskey.

5

Taxation and Regulation

The distilling industry in the United States had, since its inception, been free of government regulation. And, until the 1860s, the federal government had, as we have seen, imposed taxes on the distilling industry for only two brief periods—1791–1802 and 1814–1817—both times to pay off the debts it had incurred waging war against Great Britain. All that would change with the outbreak of another war, the American Civil War. The excise tax on distilled spirits would be reimposed, and federal regulations would be put in place to ensure that those taxes were paid. In fact, distilling soon became the most regulated industry in the United States, and the taxes levied on it represented the largest source of income for the federal government until the creation of an income tax in 1913.

In August 1862, the federal government passed a $0.20 per proof gallon (i.e., one gallon of hundred-proof whiskey) excise tax on distilled spirits. As the war continued, the cost to the government increased, and, thus, the tax was increased, first to $0.60 per proof gallon in March 1864, next to $1.50 per proof gallon in July 1864, and then to $2.00 per proof gallon in January 1865.[1] The original whiskey tax was paid as soon as the spirit left the still. But the law was changed in 1864 to allow a three-month bonding period (long enough for the wood to soak) before the tax was imposed.

After the war ended, the debt remained, and so did the tax on spirits. In July 1868, the government did offer some relief. This came in the form of a lowered tax rate—$0.50 per proof gallon—and a one-year bonding period for aging whiskey. The newly barreled whiskey was placed in a government-bonded warehouse for a year. After that year, "gaugers"—employees of the Internal Revenue Service—would measure the proof gallons in each barrel and only then determine the amount of tax owed, meaning that the distiller was no longer taxed on the liquid absorbed by the barrel.

However, the gaugers were guided in their determinations by an official manual that established a priori the amount of liquid that should be in a barrel after a year. All barrels were charged at least that amount, even if they actually contained less liquid, and barrels that contained more that the official amount were charged correspondingly more. For the government the situation was win-win. For the distillers it was cause for dissatisfaction. When the tax was increased to $0.70 per proof gallon in August 1872, many distillers began looking for a way to get around the system. The method they ultimately devised—collusion with the gaugers—led to the "Whiskey Ring" scandal of 1875.

The way in which the scam worked was that the distiller

Proof Gallon

The federal excise tax is based on a "proof gallon" of spirits. By definition, a proof gallon is one gallon of one-hundred-proof spirits at sixty-eight degrees Fahrenheit. The temperature is important because the alcohol will expand or contract with variation in temperature. A distiller could lower the volume of alcohol for tax purposes by simply chilling the liquid a few degrees in the storage vat before bottling. Then, by letting the alcohol warm and expand before bottling, the distiller would have many extra gallons of tax-free bourbon to sell.

The proof gallon is the standard tax unit applied to distilled spirits. This means that one gallon of 80-proof whiskey is taxed at 80 percent of the current rate and that one gallon of 110-proof whiskey is taxed at 110 percent of the current rate.

would make a full day's run of whiskey but the gauger would record only half of it. The distiller would then sell the non-bonded whiskey, on which he had paid no tax, at the same price as he would have charged had he actually paid the appropriate tax, and he and the gauger would split the profit. This arrangement had the further advantage to the distiller of allowing him to cut the price he charged for whiskey on which he had paid tax since he could make up the difference with what he had earned on the tax-free product.

The scandal broke shortly after the March 1875 excise tax increase—to $0.90 per proof gallon—when Benjamin H. Bristow, the secretary of the Treasury, discovered the widespread fraud that was taking place. In May 1875, the government seized sixteen distilleries in the Midwest and arrested 240 people, including distillers, gaugers, and other government employees. In fact, the scandal reached as high as O. E. Babcock, President Grant's personal secretary. All the defendants faced charges of tax fraud and corruption.

The trials began in October 1875 in a courtroom in Jefferson, Missouri. Ultimately, Babcock was acquitted. (He would go on to write a tell-all book implying Grant's involvement in the scandal, the money involved having supposedly been used to finance the president's reelection campaign.) Still, over one hundred convictions were obtained and over $3 million in taxes recovered. And the distilling industry was subjected to increased regulation.

Bonded warehouses were now outfitted with two locks on their doors. The gauger had the key to one lock, the distiller the key to the other, and neither could open the warehouse without the other being present. Further, distilleries could contain no concealed pipes so that the gauger could ensure that no whiskey was being diverted. Finally, accurate records had to be kept on the amount of grain coming into the distillery and the amount of whiskey being made. The gaugers' manual gave figures for how much whiskey could be produced per bushel of grain. Any discrepancies uncovered were immediately investigated. The government was determined to collect its taxes and avoid another scandal.

The distillers were not in principle opposed to regulations and taxes, which discouraged distilling on a small scale and favored larger producers with more capital. In fact, in some in-

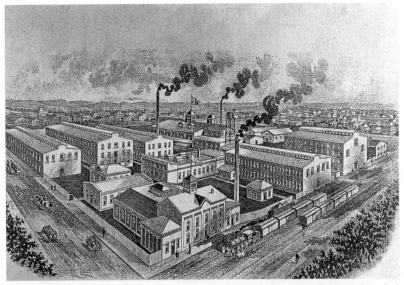

Belmont and Astor Distilleries in Louisville, Kentucky, with their bonded warehouses, ca. 1890. (Courtesy United Distillers Archive)

stances they even encouraged increased regulation. For example, because whiskey generally was not sold until it was three years old, in 1879 they arranged through their representatives in Washington, DC, to have the bonding period increased from one year to three. This move actually saved them money since, along with the liquid absorbed by the wood, evaporation also claims roughly 3 percent of a barrel's contents each year.

Nevertheless, taxes and regulations took their financial toll on distillers, especially after 1894, when the tax increased to $1.10 per proof gallon and the bonding period increased to eight years (where it would remain until the 1950s). Also, straight whiskey distillers—producers of aged whiskey—had since the end of the Civil War been facing increased competition from producers of rectified whiskey, who often made what they passed off as ten-year-old whiskey in a single day.

Angel's Share

When whiskey is being aged, evaporation through the pores of the oak barrel staves changes the proof of the whiskey. The degree to which the proof of the whiskey changes depends on where the whiskey is stored in the warehouse. If it is on one of the upper floors, the proof will increase with age; if it is on one of the lower floors, the proof will decrease with age. There is a point in the middle where the proof does not change. This change in proof is driven by heat. On the upper levels of the warehouse, where the temperature can be over one hundred degrees Fahrenheit in the summer, both alcohol and water vaporize, pressure builds up in the barrel, and water molecules, which are smaller than alcohol molecules, pass through the pores of the wood at a greater rate than do alcohol molecules, thus raising the proof of the whiskey. On the lower levels, where the temperature is much cooler—often in the midseventies even on a hot summer day—thanks to the updraft created by the rising hot air, more alcohol than water will vaporize, and more alcohol passes through the wood pores, thus lowering the proof of the whiskey.

(It should be noted that many rectifiers made a quality product.) This flooding of the market with cheap rectified whiskey—much of it foreign in origin—led to declining straight whiskey prices.

The overproduction of whiskey, combined with the depression set off by the Panic of 1873, eventually forced many straight whiskey distillers into bankruptcy. The Pepper family was one such victim, selling the Old Oscar Pepper Dis-

The Whiskey Trust

The end of the nineteenth century saw the organization of "trusts" or monopolies on goods in order to control prices. The whiskey industry was not immune to this trend. In May 1877, the Distillers' and Cattle Feed Trust was formed. It was headquartered in Peoria, Illinois, and eventually encompassed sixty-five distilleries in several states, but mostly in Illinois and western and central Kentucky. It succeeded in controlling a large amount of whiskey production, but never enough to actually control the price of whiskey. There were simply too many distilleries making whiskey, and many of them were opposed to the idea of a trust. In the 1890s, the trust became the target of state and federal government antitrust actions. It would eventually be broken into three companies—Kentucky Distilleries and Warehouse Co., American Spirits Manufacturing Co., and Standard Distilling and Distributing Co. of America—under the parent company Distillers' Securities Corp. It survived in this form until Prohibition. At the end of Prohibition, it emerged as National Distillers Corporation. (See William L. Downard, *Dictionary of the History of the American Brewing and Distilling Industries* [Westport, CT: Greenwood, 1980], 213–14.)

tillery to the firm Labrot and Graham in 1878. Another was E. H. Taylor, who sold his OFC (or Old-Fashioned Copper) Distillery, which he had purchased in 1870, to Gregory and Stagg, a whiskey wholesaler based in St. Louis. Taylor eventually formed the firm E. H. Taylor Jr. and Sons and became a champion of straight whiskey and an active crusader against the ills of overproduction.

By the 1890s, the rectifiers, who continued to pass their product off as aged Kentucky bourbon, effectively controlled the whiskey market. In order to reclaim their fair share of the market, straight distillers began lobbying the federal government for a bottled-in-bond act. The concept of bottling in bond refers to spirits that have been produced and bottled in accordance with a set of legal regulations meant to ensure authenticity and quality. The regulations signed into law as the 1897 Bottled-in-Bond Act were that the spirit must be at least four years old, have been bottled at one hundred proof, be the product of one distillery and one distiller in one season, and be unadulterated (only pure water could be added) and that the labels on both the bottle and the shipping case must clearly identify the distillery where it was distilled and, if different, the distillery where it was bottled.[2] Bonded whiskeys are, thus, distinct from straight whiskeys, which can be combinations of different bourbons made at different times and in different places.

Opposition to the bottled-in-bond legislation was strong. The producers of rectified whiskey claimed that it singled out straight whiskey—at least a certain type of straight whiskey—and gave the distillers an unfair advantage in the marketplace. The testimony before Congress of the rectifier Isaac Wolfe Bernheim is typical of the opposition. Bernheim argued that, because the name of the distiller had to be placed on both the bottle and the shipping case, even if the spirit was being made for another company, and because the practice of marrying different whiskeys was disallowed, the law would give the distillers an unfair advantage: "The blender of spirits

Old Taylor
bottled-in-bond
bourbon.
(Author's
collection)

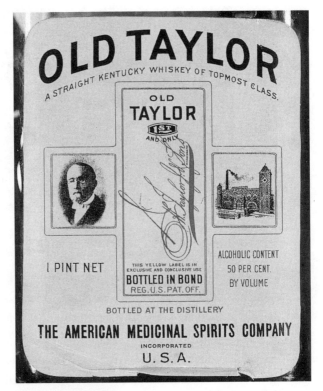

Isaac Wolfe Bernheim. (Courtesy
United Distillers Archive)

Bottling line at the Old Judge Distillery, Frankfort, Kentucky, ca. 1903. (Courtesy United Distillers Archive)

receives no protection. The distillers, particularly those from Kentucky, intend and will, with the help of the government, be encouraged to monopolize the business." He pointed out that the distillers had already attempted to bail themselves out of the consequences of what they saw as overproduction (and the rectifiers saw as healthy competition) by calling on the government to establish ever-longer bonding periods: "Distillers have called on Congress so liberally, that, like the helpless child, he constantly looks to the law making powers at Washington and in Kentucky, to rectify blunders and mistakes for which he alone should remedy." The distillers should, he felt, have stayed out of the bottling business and simply sold to those firms that were rectifying whiskey.[3]

In the event, the distillers presented the counterargument

Early Legal Challenge to the Rectifiers

The first legal challenge to the rectifiers came not from American distillers but from the government of Japan, which in 1869 objected to the practice of imported rectified whiskey being advertised as straight whiskey. The case ultimately came before the Ohio Circuit Court, the presiding judge, Alphonso Taft (the father of William Howard Taft), ruling that a product containing neutral spirits could not be called *whiskey*. While the decision did nothing to change U.S. law—the rectifiers continued to do business as usual—it did set a legal precedent that would influence the regulation of whiskey under the 1906 Pure Food and Drug Act.

that the law would ensure the purity of American-produced whiskey and help protect it from competition by Canadian bottled-in-bond whiskeys. Their coalition, led by the Kentuckians Thomas Jones of the Kentucky Distillers' Association, Edmund Taylor, the son of E. H. Taylor Jr., and James G. Carlisle, the secretary of the Treasury, won the day. President Grover Cleveland signed the bill into law on March 3, 1897, the day before the newly elected William McKinley was sworn in as president.

It took a number of years for the concept of bottled-in-bond whiskey to become well-known among the general public, even though public attention had been first drawn to the practice by Hiram Walker and Sons' 1893 Chicago World's Fair exhibit, which spotlighted the Canadian bottled-in-bond law, which had been passed in 1883. In fact, the passing of the Bottled-in-Bond Act went almost unnoticed until the 1904 Louisiana Purchase Exposition, where one feature of the Kentucky Building was a display sponsored by Kentucky distillers explaining the difference between bonded and nonbonded whiskey. From that time until Prohibition, sales of bottled-in-bond whiskey improved every year.

The war between the distillers and the rectifiers was not yet over, however. The two groups crossed swords again over the passage of the 1906 Pure Food and Drug Act. The act had been prompted by the recent work of those investigative journals known as *muckrakers* who exposed the dangers to which the practices of many companies in the food and drug industries exposed consumers. Whiskey, which fell under its purview, was defined in it as straight whiskey. All other products were imitations or compounds and should be labeled as such. This set the stage for a fight that would last over three years.

The rectifiers challenged this definition of whiskey. They argued not only that their whiskey was whiskey but also that it was the most pure form of whiskey, straight whiskey being higher in congeners and fusel oils, many of which were poisonous. Canadian and British producers joined in the challenge since, if the definition were upheld, almost all Canadian and Scotch whiskey exported to the United States would have to be labeled as imitation. Straight whiskey producers countered that the rectifiers did, in fact, add substances to their products, that many of these substances were newly developed, that the long-term effects of these substances on the human body were unknown, and that even some of the more familiar substances (such as sulfuric acid) were known to be harmful.

Pure Food and Drug Act

President Theodore Roosevelt (1858–1919) was a progressive-minded president who sought social reforms through government. One of these reforms was the Pure Food and Drug Act of 1906, which prevented the "manufacture, sale, or transportation of adulterated or misbranded or poisonous or deleterious foods, drugs, medicines and liquors" (William L. Downard, *Dictionary of the History of the American Brewing and Distilling Industries* [Westport, CT: Greenwood, 1980], 155). The act covered interstate and foreign commerce and had an impact on the spirits industry worldwide since, to sell their products in the United States, distillers had to follow the regulations established by the act.

These arguments were made before the courts and in magazines and newspapers around the country. Various interest groups took sides, the Women's Christian Temperance Union, for example, siding with the straight whiskey distillers because straight whiskey was at least an all-natural product and, thus, the lesser and safer of two evils. But it took three years for the issue to be settled.

In those three years the debate became so heated that President Taft agreed to make a decision on the issue. The two sides' chosen representatives argued their cases before him, and in December 1909 he released his decision. Neutral spirits could be used in whiskey as long as they were *grain* neutral spirits; neutral spirits made from fruit or molasses were forbidden. Whiskey made by flavoring neutral spirits had to be labeled *blended*. Straight whiskey could be labeled as such, and descriptors such as *bourbon* and *rye* could be used to identify the dominant grain. Distillers of straight whiskey could also use the descriptor *aged in wood,* but, interestingly, so could Canadian Club, which was a mixture of neutral spirits and straight whiskey that had been aged in wood. Canadian Club was the only brand mentioned by name in the decision.

At the beginning of the nineteenth century, there was no need to ask the question, What is whiskey? The answer was obvious. Whiskey was spirits distilled from fermented grain. By the end of the nineteenth century, however, the question *What is whiskey?* was being asked—and with increasing urgency. Was it straight whiskey? Was it blended whiskey? Or was it compound or imitation whiskey? The answer finally turned out to be: all of the above. And the distinctions set down in 1909 are followed faithfully today.

6

Prohibition and
the Bourbon Industry

The Eighteenth Amendment to the Constitution, which placed a national ban on the sale, manufacture, and transportation of alcohol and ushered in the Prohibition Era (1920–1933), had its origins in the social activism surrounding the Second Great Awakening, the religious revival that swept the United States during the early years of the nineteenth century. Fueled by a newly reawakened evangelical fervor, scores of men and women ardently championed such causes as the abolition of slavery, women's suffrage, and prohibition.

The first, tentative step toward nationwide prohibition was taken with the so-called Maine Laws, a series of state legislative acts prohibiting (with only a few exceptions, e.g., medicinal purposes) the sale of alcohol adopted first in Maine in 1851 and in twelve other states by 1855. The laws were highly unpopular, especially among the working classes and immigrants, and consequently were soon repealed. But, as long as they remained on the books, people busied themselves devising ways around them. One of the most popular was the "blind tiger," the earliest form of the speakeasy. The owner of such an establishment would charge customers to see an attraction (usually some exotic kind of animal) and then serve them a complimentary drink.

The setback was only temporary, however, and the temperance movement continued to gain in momentum. Temperance organizations played a key role in the march toward Prohibition. Most prominent in the late nineteenth century were the Women's Christian Temperance Union (WCTU), founded in 1873 under the leadership of first Annie Wittenmyer and then Frances Willard, and the Anti-Saloon League, founded in 1893 by the Protestant minister H. H. Russell. The WTCU sought to suppress the liquor trade and promote total abstinence from the use of alcohol. The Anti-Saloon League focused more on the evils of saloon culture—which was associated with corrupt politics and indulgence in vice—than on the individual drinker. These fundamentally religious organizations found an unlikely ally in wealthy business owners, whose very secular agenda was the promotion of sobriety among their workers as a means to increased production and, thus, increased profits.

The alcohol industry did mount a resistance movement of sorts. The only organized defense came from the beer industry, which encompassed not only the breweries that produced the beer but also the saloons and taverns (most owned by the breweries) that sold it. Those saloons and taverns mostly catered to the country's growing German-American population, and the industry's defense (mostly in newspaper

Carry Nation

Carry Nation was born in Kentucky on November 25, 1846. Her first husband was an alcoholic, and this inspired her to campaign against the liquor industry. In December 1900, she raised her hatchet for the first time at the Carey Hotel in Wichita, Kansas. She would use her trademark to smash up saloons until her death in 1911. Nation was a member of the Women's Christian Temperance Union but not part of it leadership. Many people on both sides of the issue saw her as a loose cannon and did not take her seriously. Henry Watterson—no fan of Prohibition—wrote about her death in the July 13, 1911, *Louisville Courier-Journal*: "Did she really suffer from the hysteria into which she threw herself, or enjoy the excitement and notoriety? Who shall tell? Poor, old hag! Peace to her ashes. Witches of the blasted heath, spirits of dead priestess of pagan fable—maybe the soul of Meg Merrilies herself—attended her wanderings from Dan to Beersheba, which she did not find all barren, and they will e'en follow here to her grave. Born in Kentucky, 'twas fitting that she should die in Kansas" (Arthur Krock, *The Editorials of Henry Watterson* [Louisville: Louisville Courier-Journal Co., 1923], 219).

editorials), thus, painted the temperance movement as an attack on German heritage and culture, which at that point constituted a political liability. The whiskey industry effort was, unfortunately, less organized, owing to the continuing conflict between the straight whiskey distillers and the rectifiers. Individual attempts were mounted. George Garvin Brown of Brown-Forman, for example, published the book *The Holy Bi-*

ble Repudiates "Prohibition" (1910), a compendium of Bible passages "proving that the Scriptures commend and command the temperate use of alcoholic beverages."[1] Other distillers wrote letters to newspapers and trade magazines. But the effort extended no further.

It is possible that Prohibition could have been avoided had there been some support in the alcohol industry for social and economic reforms. But most insiders took it for granted that Congress would never enact temperance legislation and, thus, that reform need not be directly addressed. In the meantime, the temperance movement was concentrating its efforts not on the national level but on the local. Campaigners would push for "local-option" votes that would turn first a neighborhood, next a precinct, then a city or county, and finally a state dry. By the early years of the twentieth century, a number of states had indeed gone dry, among them Georgia (1907), Mississippi and North Carolina (1908), Tennessee (1910), West Virginia (1912), Virginia (1914), Arkansas and South Carolina (1915), and Michigan, Montana, South Dakota, Nebraska, and Utah (1916).

Prohibition became a foregone conclusion when, on April 6, 1917, the United States entered the First World War. No longer was it a political liability to attack German heritage and culture. More importantly, at a time when women did not have the vote and the Eighteenth Amendment had left Congress and gone to the states for ratification, the wartime draft sent close to three million eligible voters overseas, rendering those who were so inclined incapable of voting against prohibition. Finally, the government enacted a temporary "wartime prohibition"—limiting distillation to industrial alcohol for the war industry—that was extended at war's end because Congress was confident that the Eighteenth Amendment was going to pass.

The Eighteenth Amendment was ratified on January 16, 1919. It reads in part: "After one year from the ratification of this article the manufacture, sale, or transportation of intoxicating liquors within, the importation thereof into, or the exportation thereof from the United States and all territory subject to the jurisdiction thereof, for beverage purposes, is hereby prohibited." Notice that the *use* of alcohol—in whatever form—was not prohibited. Citizens were permitted to own and drink spirits (wine and beer would only later be included). They simply could not manufacture, sell (or buy), or transport "intoxicating liquors."

The National Prohibition Act, also known as the Volstead Act, was enacted to carry out the intent of the Eighteenth Amendment. It regulated the commercial production of alcohol for scientific and medical purposes and allowed the domestic production, for personal use, of up to two hundred gallons total of wine and/or cider per year. The Eighteenth Amendment came into force on January 16, 1920. In June 1920, the Supreme Court upheld the constitutionality of the Eighteenth Amendment. Prohibition was now the law of the land.

Distilleries across the United States were forced to close. Only the sale of alcohol for medicinal purposes remained legal, and only six companies were licensed to supply one-hundred-proof bonded spirits for those purposes: the Schenley Distillers Corporation, the American Medicinal Spirits Company (later the National Distillers Product Co.), James Thompson and Brother (later the Glenmore Distilleries Co.), the Brown-Forman Distillery Company, Frankfort Distilleries, Inc., and the A. Ph. Stitzel Distillery. (W. L. Weller and Sons piggy-backed on the license issued to Stitzel because the same three people owned both companies.)

These companies had a very limited market and primarily serviced drugstores since pharmacists could sell medicinal spirits on the orders of a doctor, who could prescribe one pint of one-hundred-proof spirits per patient every ten days. Beyond that, their market was limited to doctors and dentists, who could purchase twelve pints of one-hundred-proof spirits a year for office use, and bakers, who could purchase twelve pints of brandy or rum a year for cooking purposes. These six distributors did manage to stay in business (and keep their brand names alive), but just barely. Glenn Walsh, Stitzel-Weller's control state manager, would later recall that Julian Van Winkle (of W. L. Weller and Sons) "would chuckle when he talked about the distillers having lunch together at the Pendennis Club": "He said they would sit around the table and lie about how much whiskey they had sold—an absurd amount of barrels. You could buy whiskey only if you had a prescription. It was a limited market. It was a very tough time."[2]

Despite their closure, the distilleries themselves were not destroyed, nor were the spirits aging in their warehouses confiscated, at least not initially. But in 1922, prompted by the increasing amounts of whiskey that had been disappearing from the warehouses, the government created a system of "consoli-

Prescription for medicinal whiskey. (Courtesy United Distillers Archive)

dation warehouses," fewer warehouses enabling more effective oversight.

The Bottled-in-Bond Act was thrown into complete disarray. Even blended whiskey was being put into bond, and, anyway, the bonding period of eight years had become irrelevant since taxing whiskey that distillers could not sell proved impractical. (By the end of Prohibition [1933], bonded bourbon as old as eighteen years was being sold in the medicinal market.) The tax stamp with distillation and bottling dates continued to be used, the distiller and bottler continued to be identified, and the whiskey had to have been bottled at one hundred proof, but the remainder of the act's provisions were rendered supererogatory. Most states allowed spirits to be marketed only in pint bottles, though there were exceptions, so the vast majority of whiskey was sold in wooden cases containing forty-eight pint bottles and sealed with a gauger's mark.

As the years passed, the medicinal whiskey license holders began running out of their pre-Prohibition stocks of whiskey. This led to industry consolidation as, for example, Brown-Forman purchased the Early Times brand and what stocks of it remained. A. Ph. Stitzel and W. L. Weller and Sons similarly acquired Old Fitzgerald. Sometimes the stocks alone would be sold to be marketed under the purchaser's brand (the labeling would reflect this). And, in cases where distillers were anxious to market their product before age ruined it but were unwilling to sell either their brand or their stocks, the license holders would act as intermediaries, holding the barrels in their warehouses, charging for labor and the material cost of bottling, and earning a modest commission (about $1.00 per case) on the sale. This arrangement obtained, for example, between A. Ph. Stitzel and W. L. Weller and the brands Henry McKenna, Old Charter, Cascade, and Waterfill and Frazier. Such ventures were not highly profitable, but they kept companies in business.

Still, no distiller's stocks could last forever. Recognizing the need to replenish supplies, in 1928 the government passed an exemption to the Volstead Act that allowed distillers to resume normal operations, albeit to a limited extent. Beginning in 1929, the six license holders were allowed to manufacture three million gallons of whiskey between them. Brown-Forman no longer had an operating distillery—its distillery was outdated when Prohibition hit and was sold for scrap—and ar-

Weller storefront on Whiskey Row in Louisville, ca. 1910. (Courtesy United Distillers Archive)

ranged for A. Ph. Stitzel to make its share of whiskey through 1929 while the White Mills Distillery on Eighteenth Street in Louisville was being rebuilt. Frankfort Distilleries was also without a distillery—for the same reason—and made a similar arrangement with Stitzel that continued until 1935, when the Stitzel-Weller Distillery was opened and Frankfort purchased the old Stitzel distillery on Story Avenue in Louisville.

Distillers and brewers were not the only segment of the population to feel the economic effects of Prohibition. Saloon, tavern, and even hotel bar employees were forced to find work elsewhere. The farmers who provided grain to the distillers and brewers lost one of their major domestic markets, and exacerbating their situation was a steep drop in grain prices in 1926 that forced them to sell their crops at a loss. Similarly affected were the manufacturers who made beer and whiskey bottles, the printers who printed beer and whiskey labels, the railroads who shipped beer and whiskey to their markets, importers of corks, the newspapers in which alcoholic beverages were advertised, the advertising agencies that designed those advertisements—the list goes on and on. The point is that Prohibition cost Americans jobs. It also cost the government tax revenue and, thus, was economically feasible only because of the passage in 1913 of the Sixteen Amendment, which established the federal income tax. Of course, medicinal spirits were still taxed, but the amount thus collected was a small fraction of what had been collected before 1920. The duty on imported wines and liquors was also lost, not to mention the income tax no longer being paid by workers who had lost their jobs.

Worse for the government in some ways was the fact that Americans soon learned to sidestep Prohibition. Speakeasies opened across the country, supplied by alcohol smuggled in from Great Britain, Cuba, and other spirit-producing nations. (A particular favorite among bootleggers was Mount Vernon rye, a pint of which mixed with four pints of one-hundred-proof neutral spirits made a very good blend, much in demand on the black market.) People who could not afford imported whiskey or rum made do with homemade gin and medicinal whiskey stretched by the addition of neutral spirits made mostly in illegal home stills.

One of the most famous suppliers of illegal whiskey was

The Real McCoy

During Prohibition, a rum-runner named William Frederick McCoy was known for the fact that he never watered his booze and that, when you purchased spirits from him, you got the genuine product. Some say that this is the origin of the phrase *the real McCoy*.

George Remus—dubbed by the press "the king of the bootleggers." Remus was born in Germany, but when he was five his parents emigrated to the United States, settling in Chicago. In his youth he helped support the family by working at a pharmacy, which he later bought. Within five years he expanded, buying another pharmacy. But he soon tired of the business and, after a stint in law school, set up what turned out to be a very successful practice. Then, with the coming of Prohibition, he saw a way to make a great deal of money—selling whiskey on the black market. He moved his business to Cincinnati to be closer to his sources and in 1920 started the Drobbatz Chemical Company, which he used to obtain permits to transfer whiskey from warehouses to his pharmacies. (The permits were easily obtained from corrupt Harding administration officials.) He would then hijack his own whiskey in transit and sell it on the black market for a greater profit than he could otherwise realize. With his newfound wealth, he also began purchasing distilleries. By 1925, when he was indicted for thousands of violations of the Volstead Act, he had gathered a fortune of $40 million and earned a reputation as a lavish entertainer.

Remus wound up spending two years in a federal prison. When he got out, he found out that his wife, Imogene, who had initiated divorce proceedings in 1927, had liquidated his assets, hiding most of the money. Still, he lived up to his reputation for extravagance, chasing down and killing Imogene as she was on her way to court to finalize the divorce. He was acquitted after mounting an insanity defense and lived out the rest of his life modestly and quietly, dying of natural causes in 1952.[3]

Remus was a supplier of aged whiskey on the black market, but not all the product sold there was of such high quality. Organized criminal gangs began to produce distilled spirits to meet the growing popular demand. Quality was not as important to them as quantity, and they bottled complete runs off stills, including the first spirits, which were cut by reputable distillers because they contained poisonous wood alcohol. Many unwary consumers were blinded or even killed, as attested by numerous newspaper stories that survive from the period.

Criminal syndicates were violent as well as unethical organizations, and the number of murders associated with the black market for alcohol increased as Prohibition went forward. But the violence was mostly between rival gangs as they fought over supplies of alcohol or territory, and the average American citizen saw nothing wrong with purchasing alcohol on the black market. In fact, most people saw the criminal distributors as modern-day Robin Hoods fighting back against a repressive and corrupt government in the person of the police. Consequently, law enforcement agencies found it difficult to suppress black market activity.

Eighteenth Amendment

The Eighteenth Amendment to the Constitution of the United States is the only amendment to limit the freedom of citizens. It is also the only amendment to have been repealed.

Clearly, the "Noble Experiment" that was Prohibition had failed. Its intent had been to create a sober and more perfect society. In reality, it did just the opposite. Arrests for drunkenness and drunken driving and instances of alcoholic insanity and death from alcoholism all increased during Prohibition.

Not surprisingly, opposition to Prohibition began to organize early. The state of New York repealed its enforcement act in 1923, and Illinois voted to modify the Volstead Act in 1926. In that same year, Montana repealed its enforcement act, and the Nevada legislature denounced Prohibition. The Association against the Prohibition Amendment was formed in 1927. And Wisconsin repealed its enforcement law in 1929.

Recognizing that the Eighteenth Amendment was a failure, at least in its current state, in May 1929 President Herbert Hoover, who in 1928 had campaigned on a platform that included support for Prohibition, created the Wickersham Commission and charged it with identifying policy initiatives that would combat the growth of organized crime. The commission's final report, released in 1931, documented widespread evasion of Prohibition and its negative effects on American society but did not recommend the repeal of the Eighteenth Amendment. Instead, the report proposed the introduction of more aggressive and extensive law enforcement efforts.

Still, opposition to Prohibition continued to grow, and, by the 1932 presidential election, which brought Franklin Roosevelt to office, both major parties were promising to repeal the Eighteenth Amendment. The Twenty-first Amendment repealing the Eighteenth was proposed by Congress in February 1933 and ratified by the states in December 1933. Its first section reads: "The eighteenth article of amendment to the Constitution of the United States is hereby repealed." But its second section stipulates: "The transportation or importation into any State, Territory or Possession of the United States for delivery or use therein of intoxicating liquors, in violation of the laws thereof, is hereby prohibited." That is, states retained essentially absolute control over alcoholic beverages, and many states remained dry. Prohibition was over—sort of.

7

The End of Prohibition and the Second World War

The thirteen long, dry years of Prohibition had taken their toll on the American distilling industry. Most distilleries were in ruins, and, of the experienced distillers who were still alive, many were too old to have any interest in starting up their businesses again. Tastes had changed too. Lighter liquors like blended whiskeys, gin, and rum had become popular. Gin and unaged white rum could be manufactured quickly, and Canadian and Scotch whiskeys and Caribbean rum had never gone out of production. Those distillers interested in resuming production would need two years to get a straight American whiskey and four years to get an aged and bonded whiskey to what was already a flooded market. They would also need to find capital in a world mired in first the Great Depression and then the Second World War.

Despite the obstacles, however, many old bourbon brand names were revived. And the distillers decided that the first order of business was some long-overdue self-regulation, a preemptive public relations effort to ensure that the idea of prohibition would remain dead. In early 1934, the first voluntary Code of Responsible Practices was approved. Among its regulations were the following:

1. We have agreed not to use radio because we think it would be bad public relations to come into the family circle and promote our products in a way which forces them on the attention of women and children.
2. We have agreed not to use pictures of women or children in our advertising for much the same reasons that we don't use radio.
3. We have agreed not to advertise in Sunday newspapers because it might be resented by many people.
4. We are forbidden to mention any of the physical effects of liquor either directly or by implication.
5. We are forbidden to use pictures of men in the uniform of our armed services or to illustrate military or naval equipment.
6. We are forbidden to mention the names or establishments of retail licenses in any consumer advertising, since that is considered an illegal service to the retailer.[1]

These regulations were followed in every state in the Union and became the basis of the Code of Responsible Practices first developed by the Distilled Spirits Council of the United States on its formation in 1973.

Individual states often placed additional restrictions on

the advertising of spirits. A 1946 training manual gives the following list of regulations common to many states:

1. Drinking scenes. This restriction stems from a belief in the minds of some commissioners that the pictures of people enjoying our products would encourage some non-drinkers to become drinkers. In general, the liquor industry is supposed to confine its appeal to people who already use some type of distilled spirits.

2. Price advertising. Several states forbid either the listing of bottle prices or any mention of price, value or economy. The commissioners in these states feel that such advertising encourages buying by people who can't afford a luxury product, and also that price advertising stimulates price wars in the trade.

3. Testimonials. Some authorities feel that a man's choice of a whiskey brand has little to do with his success as a businessman, actor or social leader and that it is unfair to imply that it does by means of endorsements and testimonials.

4. Recipes. The ban on telling people how to make mixed drinks is apparently based on a belief that recipe ads make drinking appear more attractive and therefore encourage greater consumption. Most state commissioners feel that their job is to *regulate* rather than to help *promote* the sale of liquor.

5. Holiday advertising. Few distillers would have the bad taste to use pictures of Santa Claus or religious symbols in their advertising, but many of them use some form

of seasonal copy to promote their brands as Christmas gifts. In a number of states, however, any use of the word "Christmas" is a serious violation of regulations, and in some states an illustration of a Christmas tree, holly or mistletoe is also forbidden.

6. Display material. Federal regulations prohibit a distiller from having more than $10.00 worth of display material in use to advertise his brands at any one time in a single retail establishment. Therefore expensive and attractive display devices frequently employed by advertisers in other lines of business can not be used to promote Frankfort brands if the cost exceeds the Federal limit of $10.00. In addition to this Federal restriction on the value of the display material, some states limit the cost even further and many limit the size of the display piece.[2]

The federal government also placed regulations on the liquor trade. As of 1933, sale directly from the barrel was illegal, and spirits could be sold only in standard bottle sizes: one-tenth pint, half pint, pint, four-fifths quart, and quart. The government also recognized half gallon and gallon bottle sizes, but these were allowed by only a few states. Finally, any whiskey that was to be marketed as a straight whiskey had, after March 1, 1938, to be made using brand-new charred oak barrels.[3]

Recognizing the change in consumer taste, many distillers altered their flavor profile accordingly. Before Prohibition the barrel-entry proof for bourbon was usually 100 or less.

To lighten the flavor of their whiskey, distillers simply started to raise barrel-entry proof—inching toward the Standards of Identity maximum of 110—thus taking out more of the grain oils. (The Standards of Identity, established by the Federal Alcohol Administration Act of 1936, set precise guidelines for the manufacture and aging of spirits.) Many distillers also introduced their own blended whiskeys. This strategy was particularly popular among distilleries that had stocks of pre–Prohibition era aged whiskey in their warehouses.

Immediately after Prohibition the distilling industry was made up of three types of companies. First were the companies that had been licensed to sell medicinal alcohol during Prohibition. These had some stocks of whiskey remaining, but it was over-aged and bitter. Second were the companies that had closed but had managed to hold on to their brands waiting for Prohibition to end. These had the advantage of name recognition once they got their production lines running again. Third were the start-ups. These faced the challenge of creating their own brands and winning over consumers.

The competition among these companies was fierce, and those that were not on solid financial ground, established and start-up alike, failed. The distilling industry saw an initial wave of consolidation in the 1930s as stronger distillers bought up the brands and the stocks of bankrupt companies.

Schenley Distilleries and National Distillers were the two largest American companies to emerge from Prohibition. They and the Canadian companies Seagram's and Hiram Walker became known as the "Big Four" North American distilleries.

These four companies controlled the majority of the trade in distilled spirits, domestic and imported. National Distillers owned the brands with the most name recognition—Old Crow and Old Taylor bourbons and Old Overholt and Mount Vernon rye whiskeys. Seagram's focused on blended whiskey and was known for its Crown Royal Canadian whiskey and Seven Crown American blended whiskey. Hiram Walker had Canadian Club whiskey and prepackaged cocktails to fuel its sales. Schenley would eventually become the largest of these companies and, thus, serves as a good case study of a midcentury distiller.

Schenley emerged from Prohibition with four active distilleries: the Schenley Distillery at Schenley, Pennsylvania, the Geo. T. Stagg Distillery at Frankfort, Kentucky, the James E. Pepper Distillery at Lexington, Kentucky, and the Squibb Distillery at Lawrenceburg, Indiana. With these distilleries came such respectable brands as Golden Wedding rye, James E. Pepper bourbon, Old Stagg bourbon, and Old Quaker bourbon and rye. Just before the repeal of Prohibition, Schenley had some bourbon-style whiskey made in Canada, and in 1936 it brought this aged whiskey to the United States and bottled it as Ancient Age. It now had an aged product to sell in a market still offering mostly one- and two-year-old whiskeys. In 1935, the forward-thinking company had also, despite the current shortage of product, created the Schenley International Corporation to handle the export of American whiskey and other spirits.

Schenley also began expanding during this period. It acquired the New England Distilling Company (Covington,

James E. Pepper Distillery, Lexington, Kentucky, ca. 1900. (Courtesy United Distillers Archive)

Kentucky) and its industrial rum business in 1935 and the Bernheim Distilling Company (Louisville) and its I. W. Harper, Old Charter, Belmont, and Astor brands of bourbon and rye in 1937. In 1936, it signed a deal to import Dewar's Scotch whiskey; in 1938, it purchased the trademark rights to George A. Dickel's Cascade whiskey; and it acquired the American Eagle Distillery (Phoenix, Arizona) in 1939 and the Oldtyme Distilling Corporation (Chapaze Station, Kentucky, and Cedarhurst, Maryland) with its Green River bourbon and Three Feathers blended whiskey and the Cresta Blanca Wine Company of California in 1940.

This national and, ultimately, international expansion continued in the 1940s and 1950s. The companies Schenley acquired included the John A. Wathen Distillery and the Buffalo Springs Distillery (1941); Roma Wines and the Blatz Brewery (1943); the Louisville Cooperage (1944); and the Quebec Distillers (which became Canadian Schenley, Inc.), the Fairfield Distillery, Many, Blanc and Company, and Ron Carioca Distilleries (1945). The pace of acquisition slowed after 1945, but the company continued to grow, reaching its largest extent in 1954 with the acquisition of a second Canadian distillery (in Vancouver, British Columbia) and the Park and Tilford Co. in Louisville. The company survived until it was purchased by United Distillers in 1989.

Not only established companies fared this well. Some start-ups proved equally successful. Heaven Hill, for example, was formed in 1935 by the five Shapira brothers and their partners. The brothers had no prior experience in the distilling industry, but they knew how to run a business—they owned a chain of department stores in Kentucky—and they had a solid business plan, which included hiring first Harry Beam and his son Joe to run the distillery. (The job remains in the Beam family to this day.) By the end of the Second World War the Shapira brothers had managed to acquire the entire company from their partners, and the business continues to thrive today.

Initially Heaven Hill had only its start-up brands to market: Heaven Hill and Bourbon Falls. But it also sold bulk whiskey. Liquor stores and bars desiring their own label would come to Heaven Hill and purchase the bourbon, which for a fee they could also have bottled. Heaven Hill also sold extra whiskey to distilleries in need. As the years passed, Heaven Hill built its own brands, but it also acquired brands from companies going out of business or brands that companies no longer wanted, for example, those that were of limited value because they were sold only in a particular state or region. In this way it has saved many pre-Prohibition brands from extinction while turning a profit.

Sometimes established companies merged in order to stay afloat after Prohibition. This was the case with the Stitzel-Weller Distillery, the result of a merger between W. L. Weller and Sons and the A. Ph. Stitzel Distillery. The newly formed company was in possession of a small stock of aged whiskey and some well-known brands. Still, compared to the Big Four, its share of the market was small. So the first item on its agenda was to make a product that would taste good at a young age. This was accomplished by using a mash bill developed by the Stitzel family that used winter wheat instead of rye as the small grain. The resulting bourbon proved popular and became the only type of bourbon Stitzel-Weller would make to market under its own name. It would, however, make other bourbons for third parties if the price was right. And, like Heaven Hill, it developed a business selling bulk whiskey—but to high-end organizations that wanted a private label.

Stitzel-Weller was run by Julian P. Van Winkle, Alex T. Farnsley, and A. Ph. Stitzel. Farnsley died in 1941 and Stitzel in 1947, leaving Van Winkle in control. Van Winkle was not a distiller, but he was a very good salesman and marketer who created marketing plans that would inspire future generations of distillers. These included creating new high-quality products such as barrel-proof and extra-aged bourbons and writing a newspaper and magazine column that exalted the Old

Julian Van Winkle, Alex Farnsley, and A. Ph. Stitzel sitting in the office at Stitzel-Weller. (Courtesy Sally Van Winkle Campbell)

Fitzgerald Bottled-in-Bond bourbon through folksy and comic stories.

Under Van Winkle, Stitzel-Weller focused on its own brands—Cabin Still (four years old and 90 proof), W. L. Weller Special Reserve (seven years old and 90 proof), Weller Antique (seven years old and between 107 and 114 proof), and Old Fitzgerald Bottled-in-Bond (which came in four-, six-, and eight-year-old expressions and was 100 proof). When in the 1950s the bonding period was increased from eight to twenty years, it started introducing older versions of Old Fitzgerald— eight, ten, twelve, and fifteen years.

The company thrived through the early 1960s, but a decline in bourbon sales in the late 1960s, combined with the aging of the stockholders, created a situation in which the Van

Winkle family was forced to sell its brands to Norton-Simon in 1972. (Julian Van Winkle had died in 1965.)

World War II changed the distilling industry yet again. The war effort required a great deal of high-proof alcohol. So, after the United States was drawn into the war by the attack on Pearl Harbor, the War Production Board assumed control of the distilling industry and oversaw its conversion from the production of beverage alcohol to the production of industrial alcohol. The conversion took time, and not all distilleries were capable of producing the required 190-proof alcohol. Ultimately, however, the distilling industry was responsible for 44 percent of the 1.7 billion gallons of industrial alcohol produced during the war. (The rest was produced at industrial alcohol distilleries or imported from the Caribbean Islands.)

The uses of industrial alcohol in the war effort were many. Some 126 million gallons were used to make antifreeze, essential in the cold-weather fighting in the Soviet Union and the Aleutian Islands. Another 66 million gallons were used to make tetraethyl lead, which was mixed with gasoline as an inexpensive octane booster. Seventy-five million gallons went to plastics for the aviation industry, 115 million gallons to the production of lacquer (to protect metal from rust) and insecticide for use in the South Pacific, and 30 million gallons to medical supplies. But the greatest amount of industrial alcohol went to the production of smokeless gunpowder for ammunition (200 million gallons) and synthetic rubber for tires, hoses, waterproofing, etc. (1.2 billion gallons).[4]

Schenley Distilleries offers an excellent case study of the

The Culin Device

A Schenley engineer named Curtis C. Culin, a sergeant in the army during World War II, developed a device, made from scrap iron collected from demolished German barricades, that was mounted on the front of tanks to cut their way through the hedgerows during the D-Day invasion of Normandy.

varied effects of the war on the American distilling industry. Even before war was declared, Louis Rosenstiel, the president of Schenley at the time, had recognized the coming need for high-proof alcohol and had his engineers develop a modified column still that could make high-proof alcohol less expensively (the plans for which were made available to other distilleries at no cost). Schenley was also able to put its skilled chemists to work on the production of penicillin for domestic and military use. (The process of growing the molds needed to produce penicillin was very similar to the process of growing yeast.)

Probably the most significant effect on all distilleries, however, was seen in terms of employment patterns. For one thing, because the distilleries were running around the clock to keep up with wartime demand, their labor needs increased dramatically. At the same time, many younger employees were enlisting in the armed forces or being drafted. (Schenley kept such employees on the payroll, sending their families a small paycheck each month as long as they remained on active duty.) In the face of these labor shortages the distilleries began hiring first African Americans and then women. Schenley was no exception, but it faced opposition from the labor unions, which were afraid that servicemen who were replaced by lower-paid women would not get their jobs back owing to payroll considerations.[5] Rosenstiel's solution was to guarantee that returning servicemen could have their old jobs back. Women's jobs were guaranteed only if they were working newly created shifts and only as long as those shifts were needed.

Like the rest of America, the distilling industry was faced with shortages. The glass bottles it used were redesigned to use less glass and had to be made from recycled glass. Shipping cases were reused, and new cases were made from recycled cardboard. All distilleries also received the same, set amount of grain regardless of their size. The smaller distilleries that could not produce 190-proof alcohol saw reduced profits, and this fact, combined with labor shortages, forced many of them out of business. As a result, the industry saw a second wave of consolidations. Schenley, for example, acquired the Wathen Distillery and the Buffalo Springs Distillery, among others.

There was still a market for beverage alcohol, and, while they could not brew it, distilleries could sell what stocks of aging whiskey they had in their warehouses, often resorting to producing blended whiskeys to stretch their limited stocks. The limited amount of American whiskey available was supplemented a bit by imported whiskey, but even this was hard to come by. British whiskeys, for example, were mostly stuck in warehouses, the government having confiscated distillers' trucks for military use, and much of the whiskey that distillers were able to export to the United States fell victim to German submarine warfare. Ironically, this whiskey market turned out to be an important source of revenue for the U.S. government, which capitalized on the situation by raising the whiskey tax from its 1941 level of $3.00 per proof gallon to $9.00 per proof gallon by the war's end, collecting over $6 billion in the process.[6]

When the war ended in 1945, American distillers prepared to welcome their employees back home and get back to the business of making whiskey. But they faced an unexpected delay. Pro-prohibition elements in the government tried to force an extension of the wartime limit on grain available to distillers, arguing that it was needed to feed the cattle and hogs that were needed to feed a starving world. The distilling industry successfully countered that spent mash is a better feed than unfermented grains. But it was 1946 before the production of beverage alcohol began again.

Whiskey supplies spent the next four years catching up with demand. Blended whiskey was still a very large part of the marketplace, but, as bonded whiskey came of age, its market share grew. The war had brought the nation out of its long depression, and people had discretionary income to spend on luxury items. As the 1940s turned into the 1950s, the distilling industry was once again beginning to prosper.

8

Boom and Then Bust

The 1950s was the golden age of the Kentucky bourbon industry. There were no restrictions on production—beyond sales projections—and distillers were able to offer consumers a wide variety of products at reasonable prices. These innovations were sparked by a number of different factors.

Schenley's Louis Rosenstiel perceived the outbreak of hostilities between North and South Korea as the beginning of another world war and ordered an increase in production to build up stocks before the government stepped in and once again stopped the production of beverage alcohol. He was wrong, of course, and found himself with warehouses overstocked with bourbon on which he would have to pay a huge tax bill in eight years. So he lobbied the government to increase the bonding period to twenty years. His efforts were successful, and the Forand Bill was passed in September 1958 to go into effect in July 1959.[1]

Distillers were now free to market older whiskeys. Schenley, for example, released ten- and twelve-year-old versions of

Old Charter ("the whiskey that didn't watch the clock"), a ten-year-old version of Ancient Age, and ten- and twelve-year-old versions of I. W. Harper. And Stitzel-Weller released ten-, twelve-, and fifteen-year-old versions of Old Fitzgerald. It also targeted an older market segment that remembered the pre-Prohibition whiskey that came straight from the barrel without a reduction in proof with its Weller Original Barrel Proof, a seven-year-old bourbon that initially varied in proof between 107 and 110 but eventually settled at 107.[2]

As the cold war heated up, the market for bourbon became international. Just as Scotch whiskey went global by following the armed forces of Britain to every corner of its empire, so too bourbon whiskey followed the U.S. military to its bases in South Korea, Japan, Germany, and Italy. Initially available only through base exchanges, bourbon was soon among the standard offerings of local bars catering to servicemen, giving the locals a chance to develop a taste for it as well.

American distilleries began marketing their products internationally. Schenley, for example, made I. W. Harper bourbon its international brand and brokered deals with distribution companies serving countries with an American military presence (and creating their own distribution companies where none existed). By 1966, after expanding into such Third World markets as Central and South America, I. W. Harper was being advertised in 110 countries worldwide.

Jim Beam, however, is the singular success story when it comes to international marketing. It had an initial advantage in that Jim Beam was one of the whiskeys made available by the U.S. Army in its base exchanges, and American soldiers became its unpaid salesmen. Jack Daniels gained a huge advantage when it caught on with Frank Sinatra, Dean Martin, and the rest of the Rat Pack. The growth process was slow, and the competition from the Scotch whiskey industry was fierce— the fixed notion was that bourbon was a cheap alternative to Scotch—but eventually Jack Daniel's Old No. 7 Tennessee whiskey would become the international industry leader. (Few foreign regulatory agencies recognize the difference between Tennessee whiskey, which is filtered through sugar maple charcoal before going into the barrel, and bourbon whiskey.)

Schenley of course jumped on the bandwagon of Old No. 7's growing popularity. When it was unable to acquire the Jack Daniel's Distillery (it was outbid by Brown-Forman), it launched its own brand of Tennessee whiskey. It had purchased the George Dickel Cascade bourbon brand in 1935, but, fearing the market confusion that would likely result if Cascade were brought back as a Tennessee whiskey, it launched George Dickel No. 8 and No. 12 instead.

The other big success story of the 1950s is Maker's Mark. Having sold the family distillery and its brand in the 1940s, Bill Samuels Sr. wanted to get back in the business. So he

Why "No. 8" and "No. 12"

George Dickel No. 8 and George Dickel No. 12 were released under those brand names because consumer studies showed the numbers eight and twelve to be the most popular. Neither number has anything to do with the age of the whiskey.

When you
respect a man's taste.
And value his friendship.

Maker's
(S IV) Mark
KENTUCKY STRAIGHT BOURBON
WHISKY
Old Style Sour Mash

Think of it as the uncompromised whisky. Made with an absolute concern for quality.
And an absolute disregard for the concerns of time and cost. Serve your friends Maker's
Mark, and you've told them you know they appreciate the very best. And that you
think they're worth it. Maker's Mark. It's the culmination of four generations of excellence
in the art of making Kentucky whisky.

It tastes expensive...and is.

Maker's Mark Distillery, Loretto, Ky. Ninety Proof — Fully Matured.

An advertisement for Maker's Mark. (Courtesy Jim Beam Distillery)

bought the Burkes Spring Distillery, which he renamed the
Star Hill Distillery, and set out to make a single, premium
brand of bourbon. After testing several mash bills, he settled on one made of winter wheat instead of rye.[3] He named

his bourbon after his wife's pewter collection (each piece of which had its own maker's mark), had uniquely shaped, wax-sealed bottles designed, and introduced Maker's Mark to the market in 1959. The distillery had a limited capacity, so Samuels kept the market area small. Nevertheless, Maker's Mark gained a reputation as a top-notch bourbon, in the process developing a loyal customer base that helped it retain its market share in the 1960s and beyond, even as other brands were losing theirs.

Yet another marketing innovation to sweep the distilling industry in the 1950s was holiday packaging. Some of the best designers of the day were hired to create special bottles—more like decanters and often with stoppers that doubled as jiggers. The packaging was festive—although keeping within the industry's self-imposed regulations for advertising—and often featured cocktail recipes. The effort was so successful that by the 1960s the glass decanters had been replaced by ceramic decanters, which in some markets were offered year-round. Jim Beam in particular was deeply invested in this marketing strategy, producing decanters depicting everything from cars and trucks, to animals, to famous opera characters, as well as celebrating various commemorative themes. But other distillers cashed in on the craze as well. George Dickel came out with a 110th anniversary powderhorn bottle, I. W. Harper had its bowing-man decanter with gray pants and top hat for southern markets and blue pants for northern, and Early Times released a series of decanters shaped like all fifty states of the Union. Decanters became so popular that nondistillers sometimes got in on the action by purchasing bulk whiskey and bottling it in ceramic decanters. Clubs were formed, and collecting ceramic decanters became a hobby in its own right.

The bourbon industry roared into the 1960s with a strong domestic market share and a growing international market. And things seemed only to be looking up when in 1964 the U.S. Congress recognized bourbon as "a distinctive product of the United States" just as Scotch whiskey, Canadian whiskey, and cognac were distinctive products of Scotland, Canada, and France, respectively. Its resolution stipulated that "to be entitled to the designation 'bourbon whiskey' the product must conform to the highest standards and must be manufactured in accordance with the laws and regulations of the United States which prescribe a standard of identity for 'bourbon whiskey'" and instructed that "the appropriate agencies of the United States Government . . . will take appropriate action to prohibit the importation into the United States of whiskey designated as 'bourbon whiskey.'"[4]

But the mood of the nation changed dramatically as the decade progressed. The Vietnam War created a generation of rebellious young people who rejected anything and everything their parents stood for, including their alcoholic beverage choices. They turned away from whiskey to beer and wine, vodka and tequila, the latter two being spirits that until this time had only a very small share of the American market. Irish and rye whiskey sales had already been in decline as sales of Scotch and bourbon grew steadily stronger in the 1940s and 1950s; now whiskey sales across the board plummeted.

The distilling industry was caught between a rock and a hard place. It was losing the youth market, but it feared being accused of promoting underage drinking by targeting it. Also, because of its self-regulation, it could not match the radio and television advertising that the wine and beer industries employed. And, because sales predictions had to be made four, eight, even twelve years in advance, the surprising drop-off in market share left it with warehouses overstocked with a product that was not moving. Once again, the smaller companies began to go out of business.

The bigger, better capitalized companies fared somewhat better. Schenley, for example, managed to stay afloat because it had continued to expand, in the 1950s purchasing Blatz beer and investing in such products as Canadian whiskey, rum, cordials, and wine. But expansion was not the only route to survival. Maker's Mark remained prosperous precisely because it continued to produce a high-quality product and kept its markets close to home and small. And Jack Daniel's capitalized on its reputation as the drink of choice of the rebellious Rat Pack and successfully appealed to the younger generation, becoming popular among the hard rock crowd and motorcycle clubs.

The boom had gone bust. The major players in the industry were changing as the old guard died off, and the young turks who took their place took the industry in a different direction. The American whiskey market looked bleak, but change was once again on the horizon.

9

Into the Twenty-first Century

Renewed hope came to the distilling industry in the 1980s in the form of single-malt Scotch whiskey. For over one hundred years the world had been drinking blended Scotch whiskey. But now the individual malt whiskeys that went into the blends—each of which has a very strong, individual flavor profile—were being exported and sold on the American market. The marketing strategy employed by distillers piggybacked on the 1970s vogue for wine tastings. Tastings of single-malt Scotches were promoted, hoping to increase interest both in the single malts and in the blends. The strategy worked, and sales grew, attracting media exposure and, thus, generating further sales growth.

Bourbon distillers watched these events closely, trying to figure out how they could capitalize on the popularity of single-malt Scotches. The answer was single-barrel bourbon. Elmer T. Lee, the master distiller and plant manager of the newly formed Age International, remembered that Colonel Albert Blanton, the manager of the distillery under Schenley in

Elmer T. Lee. (Courtesy D. Prather)

the 1930s and 1940s, would find a very high-quality barrel of bourbon and have its contents bottled, without blending, for use as gifts for dignitaries visiting the distillery. The Blanton's brand of single-barrel bourbon hit the market in 1984.

Age International counted on the presence of the word *single* in its advertising to generate interest in its product. But, to further expose consumers to its product, it convinced the *Lane Report,* which covered business and economic news in Kentucky, to arrange a yearly contest—a blind tasting— between Blanton's and Maker's Mark, the reigning Kentucky favorite. Blanton's won repeatedly, until Maker's Mark called foul. Evidently, the bottle of Maker's Mark used was selected at random from a liquor store shelf, whereas the Blanton's was taken from an exceptionally high-quality barrel and bottled for the occasion and, thus, not representative of what consumers would be buying.

The competition came to an end, but not before Age International had achieved its purpose—establishing the idea of a single-barrel bourbon and the Blanton's brand in consumers' minds in a way that traditional advertising could not. In time Age International introduced several other single-barrel offerings, and other distilleries would follow suit.

The Japanese economy, which had grown at an outstanding rate in the 1960s and 1970s and continued to do so in the 1980s, also paved the way for bourbon's comeback. Along with such best-selling brands as Early Times, Four Roses, Maker's Mark, and Jim Beam, Blanton's caught on in the Japanese market, selling for a very high price, and making Age International a nice profit. But the favorite was I. W. Harper.

It sold so well that Schenley pulled it from the American market in order to circumvent its profits being funneled off by the gray market—trade through channels that, while legal, are unofficial, unauthorized, and unintended by the original manufacturer (e.g., buying in bulk on the American market and reselling at a profit on the Japanese market).

The profits brought in by single-barrel brands—which sold for over $100 a bottle in Japan, a price unheard of for bourbon in the United States—spurred the development of other superpremium bourbons. Next on the scene were the so-called small-batch bourbons, mixtures of select barrels produced in limited amounts. These were the brainchild of Booker Noe, Jim Beam's master distiller. Noe had for a number of years been bottling small amounts of bourbon at barrel proof and unfiltered, first for his personal use, and later for use as gifts for industry insiders. So, when the single-barrel bourbon phenomenon caught on, all the distillery had to do was look no further than the Booker's bourbon it was already bottling.[1]

Jim Beam introduced its small-batch collection in 1992. The collection consisted of four bourbons, each with a very different flavor profile: Booker's, Basil Hayden, Baker's, and Knob Creek. Booker's is bottled at barrel proof (usually 125 or higher) and is unfiltered, allowing all the original flavor to come through, but leaving the bourbon with the unfortunate tendency to cloud when ice is added owing to the presence of vegetable oils. Basil Hayden is bottled at 80 proof and has a light flavor designed to attracted drinkers of Canadian whiskey. Baker's is bottled at 107 proof and appeals to those who

Booker Noe. (Courtesy Jim Beam Distillery)

like a heavy-bodied, high-proof bourbon. Knob Creek is bottled at 100 proof and at nine years old and appeals to those who prefer extra-aged bourbon.

Jim Beam supported the launch of its small-batch collection with an aggressive advertising campaign and even created a club for fans of these bourbons, the Kentucky Bourbon Circle. It also sent Booker Noe and the whiskey writer Paul Pacult on a nationwide tour hosting tasting events aimed at bourbon collectors. The concept caught on, and other small-batch distillers followed suit. Master distillers soon achieved rock-star status as popular spokesmen for their products.

The final category of superpremium bourbons is the extra-aged products. Older bourbons had, of course, been on the market since the nineteenth century, but it was only in the early 1990s that they really took hold in the market. Their resurgence can be attributed to the foresight of Julian Van Winkle III, the grandson of Julian "Pappy" Van Winkle of the old Stitzel-Weller Distillery. He joined his father in the business in 1977 and, after Julian Jr.'s death in 1981, added Old Rip Van Winkle, ten years old and at 90 and 107 proofs, to his portfolio of brands. Old Rip Van Winkle was made mostly with whiskey purchased from the old Stitzel-Weller Distillery, but Julian also purchased whiskey on the open market from other distilleries. One of these whiskeys was a twenty-year-old bourbon that was the last of the whiskey in the warehouses of the Old Boone Distillery in Jefferson County, from which Julian created the brand Pappy Van Winkle Family Reserve, bottled at 90.4 proof.[2] The brand immediately won acclaim and was followed by a twenty-three-year-old version. Other companies noticed the popularity of the aged bourbons and soon started to add older products to their portfolios.

Not only were these superpremium brands popular in themselves, but they also helped increase the popularity of bourbon generally by creating a trickle-down effect. Consumers started giving the standard brands another look, and bourbon sales began to stabilize. The market shares of the more expensive brands even began to increase. And the effect was not just in Japan and other overseas markets (including those of the newly opened Eastern European countries) but also in the United States.

The industry was caught somewhat off guard by these developments. Whiskey was coming back faster than had been expected, and supply was having trouble keeping up with demand. To make matters worse, Heaven Hill, Wild Turkey, and Jim Beam would lose warehouses—and a significant amount of aging whiskey—to fires around the turn of the century. The result was an even greater tightening of the market.

During the last two decades of the twentieth century, whiskey had been receiving ever-increasing media exposure. An important milestone was Michael Jackson's *World Guide to Whiskey* (1987), one of the first books to focus on whiskey tasting and heritage, which included a section on the American whiskeys, including bourbon, rye, and Tennessee. Books focusing exclusively on American whiskeys soon followed, including Mark Waymack and James Harris's *The Book of Classic American Whiskeys* (1995), Gary and Mardee Regan's *The Book of Bourbon and Other Fine American Whis-*

The Kentucky Bourbon Trail

In 1999, inspired by the growing tourism trade in California's wine country, the Kentucky Distillers' Association (KDA) created the Kentucky Bourbon Trail distillery tour, meant to encourage visitors to come to Kentucky. In 2007, the KDA developed an incentive program whereby tourists received "passports" that are to be stamped after their tour of a KDA-member distillery. When the passport has been stamped by every KDA-member distillery, it can be mailed to KDA headquarters and exchanged for a free T-shirt.

From modest beginnings in 1999, the Kentucky Bourbon Trail tour has become one of the state's most popular and unique attractions, with more than 1.7 million visitors during the period 2005–2009. In 2010, more than six thousand completed passports were mailed in from forty-nine states and twelve countries to be exchanged for T-shirts, more than doubling the previous year's record total.

keys (1995) and *The Bourbon Companion: A Connoisseur's Guide* (1998), and Jim Murray's *Classic Bourbon, Tennessee and Rye Whiskey* (1998).

The periodical press also took increased notice of the American whiskey industry. For example, 1992 saw the inaugural issue of John Hansell's *Malt Advocate* magazine, which was, and still is, mostly focused on beer and malt whiskeys but does occasionally cover American whiskeys, as does the Scotch whiskey–oriented *Whisky Magazine,* which debuted in 1999. But it was the *Bourbon Country Reader,* Chuck Cowdery's self-published newsletter, that was the first publication to be devoted exclusively to American whiskey. Before launching the *Reader,* Cowdery had written, produced, and directed the PBS documentary *Made and Bottled in Kentucky* (1992), which generated enough interest to convince Cowdery that the time was ripe to launch his newsletter. Both projects proved popular with the whiskey-drinking public, and the *Reader* continues to be published today. The *Bourbon Review* followed a number of years later, created in 2009 by four young men from Kentucky who saw a need for a *Malt Advocate*–type magazine dedicated to bourbon.

This period also saw the rise of bourbon tourism. The trend began among the Japanese, but the growth of "whiskey events" targeting tourists generated interest at home as well as abroad. The first big whiskey event was the 1992 Bardstown–Nelson County Tourist and Convention Commission–sponsored Kentucky Bourbon Festival. The festival grew quickly but failed to do much to either educate people about or promote bourbon, evolving into what is now largely a street party for the locals. Still, reporters from around the world are routinely in attendance. Then, in 1998, *Malt Advocate* entered the fray, sponsoring a one-day tasting called WhiskyFest. Master distillers from around the world were in attendance, promoting their products: single-malt and blended Scotch, Irish, Japanese, American, and Canadian whiskeys. WhiskyFest proved so popular that it is now held three times a year in three different locations: Chicago, San Francisco, and New York City.

Anchoring the bourbon tourism industry is the Oscar Getz Museum of Whiskey History in Bardstown. Oscar Getz, the owner of the Barton Distillery, spent fifty years amassing

The Urban Bourbon Trail

Unable to offer a distillery tour of Louisville, but with so much other bourbon heritage to exploit in the city, in 2006 the Louisville Convention and Visitors Bureau launched a marketing initiative promoting the city as the "Gateway to Bourbon Country." In 2007, it opened a new visitors' center, which included an exhibit by the Kentucky Distillers' Association promoting the Kentucky Bourbon Trail. It began to host events such as bourbon-themed dinners at local restaurants and, in 2008, after canvassing the many bars in the city that offered wide selections of bourbon, launched the Urban Bourbon Trail. As with the Kentucky Bourbon Trail, passports are issued that can be stamped at participating bars. (To participate, bars must keep at least fifty different bourbons in stock and employ staff members knowledgeable about bourbon.) Completed passports can be exchanged for a T-shirt. By 2011, thousands of people from around the world had completed their passports.

a collection of rare artifacts and documents—dating from the precolonial period to the post-Prohibition period—concerning the American whiskey industry. In the 1960s, he opened a small museum on the grounds of his distillery. On his death in 1983, his widow donated his collection to the city of Bardstown, which opened the Getz Museum in 1984.

By far the most significant exposure that whiskey would receive, however, would be via the Internet. Surprisingly, the distilling industry was slow to capitalize on it, and the very first websites devoted to whiskey were created by fans, who offered such content as commentary on their own collections and descriptions of their experiences touring distilleries. These early sites were not interactive, and the flow of information went only one way: from the site owner to the site user. This changed in 1999 when Straightbourbon.com, which had been founded two years earlier, added a discussion feature allowing users to post and discuss questions on an ever-increasing number of topics. Other independent forums—such as Bourbonenthusiast.com and Bourbondrinker .com—followed, as, finally, did official websites for the various distilleries. Bourbon marketing had fully embraced twenty-first-century technology.

The first decade of the twenty-first century brought to the distilling industry an exciting idea—that of the "craft distiller" who, working with a small still, would make his own spirits for sale in the market. By May 2010 over seven hundred licenses had been granted to small distilleries in the United States alone. The artisan distillers that ran them were making everything from vodka to rum to malt, rye, and bourbon whiskeys. The Willett Distillery in Bardstown, for example, was established with the idea of crafting bourbon to individual customers' needs. Other companies experimented with bourbon styles. Buffalo Trace introduced several barrel-strength, unfiltered whiskeys as well as its Experimental Collection, 375-milliliter bottles at premium prices. Brown-Forman started bottling a yearly edition of Old Forester Birthday Bourbon (commemorating George Garvin Brown's birthday in September), the yearly batches picked because they highlighted a flavor found in Old Forester. And Jim Beam and other distilleries experimented with finishing bourbon in wine barrels.

The hope is that these craft distillers can do for the distilling industry what the microbreweries did for the American beer industry and renew interest in fine whiskeys with robust tastes.

Acknowledgments

There are many people who deserve acknowledgment for this book. There are the people who started me on my career in distilling history at United Distillers: Nicholas Morgan, Chris Morris, Mike Wright, and Edwin Foote. Flaget Nally and Mary Hite and all the other ladies at the Oscar Getz Museum of Whiskey History. All my other friends in the industry such as Al Young, Larry Kass, Mark Brown, Julian Van Winkle III and his sister Sally Van Winkle Campbell, Lincoln Henderson, Drew Kulsveen, Jimmy Russell, Elmer T. Lee, and all the others who would answer questions for me. There are people at the Filson Historical Society such as Jim Holmberg, Jacob Lee, Robin Wallace, Sarah Jane Poindexter, and the others in Special Collections who would cover my shifts when I took days off to do some research. There are my friends such as John Lipman, Howie Stoopes, and Timothy Stephen who would read chapters and give me feedback. Finally, there is Laura Sutton, who got me started on the book, and Nancy Stephen, who was kind enough not only to read the manuscript but also to give valuable feedback and to keep me to a timetable.

Notes

1. Farmer Distillers and the Whiskey Rebellion

1. Miscellaneous Henry Clay Papers, Filson Historical Society, Louisville.

2. Eli Huston Brown III Papers, Filson Historical Society.

3. Catherine Carpenter Family Papers, Kentucky Historical Society, Frankfort.

4. William Hogeland, *The Whiskey Rebellion: George Washington, Alexander Hamilton, and the Frontier Rebels Who Challenged America's Newfound Sovereignty* (New York: Scribner, 2006), 69.

5. Jon C. Miller, *The Federalist Era: 1789–1801* (New York: Harper & Row, 1960), 159.

6. Weller Family Papers, Filson Historical Society.

7. J. Stoddard Johnston, *Memorial History of Louisville from the First Settlement to the Year 1896* (New York: American Biographical Publishing Co., 1897), 283.

2. The Origin of Bourbon Whiskey

1. Reuben Thomas Durrett, *The Centenary of Kentucky*, Filson Club Publication no. 7 (Louisville, 1892), 79.

2. The recipe can be found in the Fenley-Williams Family Papers, Filson Historical Society.

3. Henry G. Crowgey, *Kentucky Bourbon: The Early Years of Whiskeymaking* (Lexington: University Press of Kentucky, 1971), 138.

4. Richard H. Collins, *History of Kentucky*, 2 vols. (Covington, Ky.: Collins & Co., 1874), 1:516.

5. *Frankfort Argus of Western America*, September 19, 1827, quot-

ed in Crowgey, *Kentucky Bourbon*, 136. Crowgey provides a well-accepted argument that Craig is not the inventor of bourbon.

6. *Western Citizen,* June 26, 1821, quoted in Crowgey, *Kentucky Bourbon,* 120.

7. Crowgey, *Kentucky Bourbon,* 123.

8. *Western Citizen*, August 30, 1861.

9. Letter to John Corlis from his factor, June 19, 1820, Corlis-Respess Family Papers, Filson Historical Society.

10. The July 15, 1826, letter can be found in the Corlis-Respess Family Papers.

3. The Industrial Revolution and the Distilling Industry

1. Patent papers, April 27, 1869, W. A. Gaines & Co. Papers, Oscar Getz Museum of Whiskey History, Bardstown, Kentucky.

2. Frederick Stitzel, patent model, Month 00, 1879, Filson Historical Society.

3. Louisville Board of Independent Insurance Agents, Inc., 1854–1982, Filson Historical Society.

4. James E. Pepper to William F. Mitchell, November 11, 1867, Gaines Papers.

4. Distillers and Rectifiers

1. Pierre Lacour, *The Manufacture of Liquors, Wines and Cordials without the Aid of Distillation* (New York: Dick & Fitzgerald, 1863).

2. For a full discussion of the reimposition of the excise tax, see chapter 5.

3. *Louisville Daily Express,* July 7, 1862.

4. Richard Edwards, ed., *Edward's Annual Director: To the Inhabitants, Institutions, Incorporated Companies, Manufacturing Establishments, Businesses, Business Firms, etc., etc. in the City of Louisville* (Louisville: Richard Edwards, 1864–1865), 551–52.

5. William Brown to E. H. Taylor Jr., January 11, 1870, and E. H. Taylor Jr., n.d., press release, Taylor-Hay Family Papers, Filson Historical Society.

5. Taxation and Regulation

1. Oscar Getz, *Whiskey: An American Pictorial History* (New York: David McKay, 1978), 189.

2. William Bennett, "Forty Years of Bottled in Bond," *American Wine and Liquor Journal*, March 31, 1937.

3. I. W. Bernheim, "Reasons Why H.R.8582, to Allow Bottling of Distilled Spirits in Bond, Should Not Pass," January 7, 1897, Bernheim Family Papers, University of Louisville Archives.

6. Prohibition and the Bourbon Industry

1. George G. Brown, *The Holy Bible Repudiates "Prohibition": Compilation of All Verses Containing the Words "Wine" or "Strong Drink," Proving That the Scriptures Commend and Command the Temperate Use of Alcoholic Beverages* (Louisville: G. G. Brown, 1910).

2. Sally Van Winkle Campbell, *But Always Fine Bourbon: Pappy Van Winkle and the Story of Old Fitzgerald* (Louisville: Limestone Lane, 1999), 38.

3. William A. Cook, *King of the Bootleggers: A Biography of George Remus* (Jefferson, NC: McFarland & Co., 2008).

7. The End of Prohibition and the Second World War

1. *The Book of Frankfort* (New York: Frankfort Distilling Co., 1946), 32.

2. Ibid., 32–33.

3. *Liquor Marketing and Liquor Advertising* (New York: Bretzfield, Henry, Abelard-Schuman, 1955), 216.

4. *The Record of the Alcoholic Beverage Industry in World War II* (New York: Distilled Spirits Institute, 1946), 11, 23–24, 27–33.

5. Uncataloged report to Louis Rosenstiel, June 1943, United Distillers Archive, Shively, Kentucky.

6. *Record of the Alcoholic Beverage Industry,* 44.

8. Boom and Then Bust

1. William L. Downard, *Dictionary of the History of the American Brewing and Distilling Industries* (Westport, CT: Greenwood, 1980), 26.

2. Stitzel-Weller Label Book, United Distillers Archive.

3. Oral History Tape, Foote, Wilson and Hawes, University of Louisville Archive.

4. Bourbon Resolution File, Schenley Papers, United Distillers Archive.

9. Into the Twenty-first Century

1. F. Paul Pacult, *American Still Life: The Jim Beam Story and the Making of the World's #1 Bourbon* (Hoboken, NJ: Wiley, 2003), 197–98.

2. Sally Van Winkle Campbell, *But Always Fine Bourbon: Pappy Van Winkle and the Story of Old Fitzgerald* (Louisville: Limestone Lane, 1999), 216.

Bibliography

Bennett, William. "Forty Years of Bottled in Bond." *American Wine and Liquor Journal,* March 31, 1937. This article gives a very good summary of the Bottled-in-Bond Act of 1897 and what the law means to the consumer.

Bernheim, I. W. *Reasons Why H.R. 8582, to Allow Bottling of Distilled Spirits in Bond, Should Not Pass.* January 7, 1897. Bernheim Family Papers, University of Louisville Archives. This is a pamphlet published by Bernheim of his testimony before Congress in opposition to the Bottled-in-Bond Act of 1897.

Bretzfield, Henry. *Liquor Marketing and Liquor Advertising.* New York: Abelard-Schuman, 1955. This book has information about the rules and regulations of the spirits industry of the 1950s.

Campbell, Sally Van Winkle. *But Always Fine Bourbon: Pappy Van Winkle and the Story of Old Fitzgerald.* Louisville: Limestone Lane, 1999. This is an excellent source for the history of the Van Winkle Family and the Stitzel-Weller Distillery.

Cecil, Sam K. *The Evolution of the Bourbon Whiskey Industry in Kentucky.* Paducah, KY: Turner, 1999. This book is the first attempt to give some history of every distillery in Kentucky. It has mistakes and is best used as a starting point for further research. However, it gives an excellent history of the Maker's Mark brand and distillery.

Collins, Richard H. *History of Kentucky.* 2 vols. Covington, KY: Collins, 1874. This is a well-respected history of the state of Kentucky.

Cook, William A. *King of the Bootleggers: A Biography of George Remus.* Jefferson, NC: McFarland, 2008. This is a very interesting biography of a Prohibition-era gangster.

Crowgey, Henry G. *Kentucky Bourbon: The Early Years of Whiskeymaking.* Lexington: University Press of Kentucky, 1971. This book is based on Crowgey's University of Kentucky doctoral thesis. It remains one of the best sources of information on early distilling in Kentucky.

Distilled Spirits Institute. *The Record of the Alcoholic Beverage Industry in World War II*. New York: Distilled Spirits Institute, 1946. This very good pamphlet describes the role of the spirits industry in the war.

Downard, William L. *Dictionary of the History of the American Brewing and Distilling Industries*. Westport, CT: Greenwood, 1980. This is an excellent source of distilling terms, brand names, and people in the industry.

Durrett, Reuben Thomas. *The Centenary of Kentucky*. Filson Club Publication no. 7. Louisville: Filson Historical Society, 1892. Durrett was one of the founders of the Filson Historical Society. He was an avid collector of historical papers and artifacts.

Edwards, Richard, ed. *Edwards' Annual Director to the Inhabitants, Institutions, Incorporated Companies, Manufacturing Establishments, Businesses, Business Firms, etc. . . . etc. in the City of Louisville for 1864–5*. Louisville: Richard Edwards, 1864–1865. The city directory for Louisville gives many vital statistics for the city of that year.

Frankfort Distilling Co. *The Book of Frankfort*. New York: Frankfort Distilling Co., 1946. This is a typical booklet published by a distiller to help train its new employees in distilling regulations.

Getz, Oscar. *Whiskey: An American Pictorial History*. New York: David McKay, 1978. This book is based on materials in Oscar Getz's personal collection. This collection is the foundation of the collection at the Oscar Getz Museum of Whiskey History in Bardstown, KY.

Hogeland, William. *The Whiskey Rebellion: George Washington, Alexander Hamilton, and the Frontier Rebels Who Challenged America's Newfound Sovereignty*. New York: Scribner, 2006. This is an excellent source for the history of the Whiskey Rebellion in Pennsylvania. It does a very good job of describing the events leading up to the rebellion to the trials after the fact.

Jackson, Michael. *The World Guide to Whisky*. Topsfield, MA: Salem House, 1987. Jackson was a well-respected expert on beer, and his treatment of whiskey was groundbreaking. The book respected whiskey as a drink to be enjoyed for its taste.

Bibliography

Johnston, J. Stoddard. *Memorial History of Louisville from the First Settlement to the Year 1896*. New York: American Biographical Publishing Co., 1897. This book helps provide an understanding of the central role that Louisville played in the distilling industry in the nineteenth century.

Krock, Arthur. *The Editorials of Henry Watterson*. Louisville: Louisville Courier-Journal Co., 1923. Henry Watterson was considered a very important political writer in his time. His editorials were well read throughout the United States.

Kroll, Harry Harrison. *Bluegrass, Belles, and Bourbon: A Pictorial History of Whisky in Kentucky*. New York: A. S. Barnes, 1967. This is an interesting book with many photographs of old distilleries and interviews with people who worked in the industry at the time the book was written.

Lacour, Pierre. *The Manufacture of Liquors, Wines and Cordials without the Aid of Distillation*. New York: Dick & Fitzgerald, 1863. A typical nineteenth-century book on rectifying spirits.

Miller, John C. *The Federalist Era: 1789–1801*. New York: Harper & Row, 1960. A very good history of the United States during the era of the Whiskey Rebellion.

Murray, Jim. *Classic Bourbon, Tennessee, and Rye Whiskey*. London: Prion, 1998. This is mostly a tasting book, but Murray does provide some brand history.

Pacult, F. Paul. *American Still Life: The Jim Beam Story and the Making of the World's #1 Bourbon*. Hoboken, NJ: Wiley, 2003. This book is mostly a marketing promotion from the company, but Pacult really does get to show his abilities with the modern-era history of Jim Beam whiskey.

Regan, Gary, and Mardee Haiden Regan. *The Book of Bourbon and Other Fine American Whiskeys*. Shelburne, VT: Chapters, 1995. This book has a very good general history of the bourbon industry and includes histories of individual brands.

———. *The Bourbon Companion: A Connoisseur's Guide*. Philadelphia: Running Press, 1998. This is mostly a tasting book, but there is some brief history and description of the distilling process.

Samuels, Bill, Jr. *Maker's Mark—My Autobiography*. Louisville: Saber, 2000. This book is written as a marketing publication but, because of that, provides an excellent look at Maker's Mark advertising.

Bibliography

Waymack, Mark H., and James F. Harris. *The Book of Classic American Whiskeys*. Chicago: Open Court, 1995. This is a tasting guide with a good section on history and individual brand histories.

Zoeller, Chester. *Bourbon in Kentucky: A History of Distilleries in Kentucky*. Louisville: Butler, 2009. This is an excellent look at individual distilleries in Kentucky, but there are mistakes and omissions, so it is best used as a starting place for research.

Index

advertising, 52, 58, 93–94, 111, 115.
    See also brand recognition
African American workers, 103
Age International, 113, 115
aging process, 19, 20, 22, 24, 39–
    40, 45, 47–48
Allen, Marshall J., 38
American Eagle Distillery, 97
American Medicinal Spirits Com-
    pany, 82
American Spirits Manufacturing
    Co., 69
Ancient Age brand, 96, 106
Anti-Saloon League, 78
A. Ph. Stitzel Distillery, 82, 84, 85,
    99
artisan distillers, 123–24
Association against the Prohibition
    Amendment (1927), 89
Astor brand, 97

Babcock, O. E., 66
Baker's brand, 116, 118
Baltimore and Ohio Railroad, 32
Bardstown–Nelson County Tour-
    ist and Convention Commission,
    121
barrels: charred oak, 19, 22, 27, 28,
    94; overview, 23; regulations for,
    94; storage of, 39; toasted, 28
Barton Distillery, 121
Basil Hayden brand, 116
Beall-Booth Family Papers, 10

Beam, Harry, 98
Beam, Joe, 98
Belmont brand, 97
Bernheim, Isaac Wolfe, 70, 72
Bernheim Distilling Company, 97
Big Four distilleries, 95–98
black market, 86–88
Blanton, Albert, 113, 115
Blanton brand, 115
Blatz Brewery, 97–98, 111
blind tiger, 78
bonded whiskey, 70–74, 83, 104,
    105
Bonfort's Wine and Spirits (maga-
    zine), 57
Booker's brand, 116
*Book of Bourbon and Other Fine
    American Whiskeys, The* (Regan
    and Regan), 119–20
*Book of Classic American Whis-
    keys, The* (Waymack and Har-
    ris), 119
Bottled-in-Bond Act (1897), 52, 70,
    73–74, 83
bottled-in-bond whiskey, 70–74, 83,
    104, 105
Bourbon Companion, The (Regan
    and Regan), 120
Bourbon Country Reader (newslet-
    ter), 120–21
bourbondrinker.com, 123
bourbonenthusiast.com, 123
Bourbon Falls brand, 98

Index

Bourbon Review (magazine), 121
bourbon whiskey. *See specific topics,*
    e.g., distilling industry; Industri-
    al Revolution; origin legends
Bradford, David, 14
brand recognition: and advertising,
    58; and counterfeiters, 58–59;
    first efforts at, 50–54; registering
    brand names, 54–57
Bristow, Benjamin H., 65–66
Brown, George Garvin, 57, 79–80,
    123
Brown, J. T. S., Jr., 57
Brown, William, 50, 53
Brown-Forman Distillery Company,
    57, 79, 82, 84–85, 107, 123–24
Buffalo Springs Distillery, 97, 103
Buffalo Trace Distillery, 123
Burkes Spring Distillery, 108
Butler, Benjamin, 50, 53

Cabin Still brand, 100
Canadian bottled-in-bond law
    (1883), 73
Canadian Club whiskey, 57, 76, 96
Canadian Schenley, Inc., 98
canal systems, 32
Carlisle, James G., 73
Carpenter, Catherine, 8
Cascade brand, 84, 97, 107
Cascade Hollow Distillery, 11
charcoal filtering, 10–11
cherry bounce, 9–10
Civil War: impact on distilling in-
    dustry, 48–49
Classic Bourbon, Tennessee and Rye
    Whiskey (Murray), 120
Clay, Cassius, 51
Clay, Green, 5
Clay, Henry, 5, 24, 43
Cleveland, Grover, 73
cochineal, 46, 48
Cock, John, 5

Code of Responsible Practices, 92
Coffey, Aeneas, 36
cognac, 20
coils for mash tubs, 38–39
Collins, Richard, 22
coloring agents, 45–48
column stills, 8, 36–38, 45
congeners, 42
consolidation warehouses, 82–83
consumer tastes, 91, 94–95
continuous stills, 8, 36–38
Coons, George, 5
cordials, 10
Corlis, John, 26, 27
cornmeal sweet mash recipe, 8–9
counterfeiting, 58–59
Cowdery, Chuck, 120–21
craft distillers, 123–24
Craig, Elijah, 21–22, 24
creosote, 46
Cresta Blanca Wine Company, 97
criminal activity during Prohibition,
    86–89
Crittenden, John J., 51
Crow, James, 40, 42–43, 52
Crowgey, Henry, 22, 24
Crown Royal Canadian whiskey, 96
Culin, Curtis C., 102
Culin device, 102
currency, 12

Davis, Joseph, 21
Davis, Samuel, 21
decanters, 109–10
Dewar's Scotch whiskey, 97
Dickel, George A., 11, 97, 107, 109
Distilled Spirits Council of the Unit-
    ed States, 92
Distillers' and Cattle Feed Trust
    (1877), 69
Distillers' Securities Corp., 69
distilling industry: Civil War impact
    on, 48–49; craft distillers, 123–

24; early technological advances, 36–44; farmer distillers, 3–11, 15, 16–17, 45; legends, 20–21; location of, 35–36; organization post-Prohibition, 95–101; and Prohibition, 81–85; taste changes of consumers, 91, 94–95; Vietnam War impact on, 110–11; World War II impact on, 101–4; World War I impact on, 80–81. *See also individual distilleries, e.g.,* Brown-Forman Distillery Company; regulations
doubler, 4
Drobbatz Chemical Company, 87
Durrett, Reuben, 21

Early Times brand, 84, 109, 115
Edward's annual directory for Louisville (1864–1865), 49–50
E. H. Taylor Jr. and Sons, 69
Eighteenth Amendment, 77, 81, 89, 90
embargoes, 27
employment: during Prohibition, 85–86; during World War II, 102–3
Enterprise (steamboat), 32
European distilleries, 16
extra-aged whiskeys, 118–19

Fairfield Distillery, 98
farmer distillers, 3–11, 15, 16–17, 45
Farnsley, Alex T., 99
Federal Alcohol Administration Act (1936), 95
federal income tax, 86
Fitch, John, 31, 32
flatboats, 33
flavoring agents, 45–46
Forand Bill (1958), 105
Forrester, William, 57
Four Roses brand, 115

Frankfort Distilleries, Inc., 82, 85
Fulton, Robert, 31

Gaines, Berry and Company, 43–44, 50, 53–54
Gaines, W. A., 43
gaugers, 64–66
Geo. T. Stagg Distillery, 96
George Dickel No. 8 brand, 107
George Dickel No. 12 brand, 107
German heritage and culture, 78–79, 80
Getz, Oscar, 121–22
Glenmore Distilleries Co., 82
Golden Wedding brand, 96
grain markets, 85–86, 103, 104
Grant, Ulysses S., 66
Green River bourbon, 97
Gregory and Stagg firm, 52, 69
grocers, 26–27

Hamilton, Alexander, 11, 13–15
hammer mills, 38
Hansell, John, 120
Harding, Warren: administration, 87
Harris, James, 119
Heaven Hill Distillery, 98–99, 119
Henry, Newton, 42
Henry McKenna brand, 84
Hermitage Distillery, 51, 53–54
Hiram Walker Distillery, 73, 95–96
Hirsch, Jacob, 15
Hogeland, William, 12
Holy Bible Repudiates "Prohibition," The (Brown), 79–80
Hoover, Herbert, 89
Hope Distillery, 15–17, 36
horse racetrack, 16

imitation whiskeys, 45–48, 67–68
industrial alcohol, 101–2, 103
Industrial Revolution, 31–44; aging process, 39–40; column stills,

Index

Industrial Revolution *(cont.)*
8, 36–38; methodology, 40, 42–
44; steam power, 31–35, 36;
technological advances, 36–44;
temperature regulation, 38–39;
warehouse innovations, 39
international markets, 96, 106–7, 119
Internet marketing, 122–23
I. W. Harper brand, 97, 106, 109,
115–16

Jack Daniel's Distillery (and brand),
11, 107, 111
Jackson, Michael, 119
James E. Pepper Distillery (and
brand), 96
James Thompson and Brother, 82
Japanese markets, 73, 115–16, 121
Jefferson, Thomas, 14
Jim Beam brand, 106–7, 115, 116,
118, 119, 124
John A. Wathen Distillery, 97
Jones, Thomas, 73

Kentucky Bourbon Circle, 118
Kentucky Bourbon Festival, 121
Kentucky Bourbon Trail distillery
tour, 120, 122
Kentucky Distilleries and Warehouse
Co., 69
Kentucky Distillers' Association
(KDA), 73, 120, 122
Knob Creek brand, 116, 118

labels, 57–58, 70, 84
Labrot and Graham firm, 69
Lacour, Pierre, 46–47
Lafayette, 24
Lane Report (news publication), 115
Lee, Elmer T., 113
Lee, Henry, 14
legislation. *See* regulations
licenses, 15

limestone water, 19, 42
Lincoln County Process, 11
Livingston, Robert, 31
local option votes, 80
Louisville, Kentucky, 33–36; distill-
eries in, 85, 98; Edward's annual
directory (1864–1865), 49–50;
marketing for, 122; Whiskey
Row, 35, 45, 51
Louisville and Frankfort Railroad,
34
Louisville and Portland Canal Com-
pany, 33–34
Louisville Convention and Visitors
Bureau, 122
Louisville Cooperage, 98

Made and Bottled in Kentucky (documentary), 121
Maine Laws, 77
Maker's Mark brand, 107–8, 111,
115
Malt Advocate (magazine), 120, 121
Manufacture of Liquors, The
(Lacour), 46–47
Many, Blanc and Company, 98
marketing: brand recognition, 50–
59; innovations, 99–100, 109,
122; international, 115–16; international markets, 96, 106–7,
119; and Internet, 122–23; media exposure, 119–21; of older
whiskeys, 105–6; and tourism,
121–22; youth market, 111
Martin, Dean, 107, 111
mash, 7–9, 16, 38–39, 42
McCoy, William Frederick, 87
medicinal use, 57, 81–84, 86, 95
Mida's Criteria (magazine), 57
millers, 6
Mitchell, John, 14
Mitchell, William F., 43, 44
Morgan, John Hunt, 51

Index

Mount Vernon brand, 86
Mount Vernon rye whiskey, 96
Murray, Jim, 120
Myers, Jacob, 21

name origination, 25–26, 27
Napoléon, Prince, 24–25
Nashville Railroad Company, 34
Nation, Carry, 79
National Distillers Corporation, 69, 95–96
National Distillers Product Co., 82
National Prohibition Act (1919), 81, 84, 89
neutral spirits, 45–47, 75–76
New England Distilling Company, 96–97
New Orleans (steamboat), 32
Noe, Booker, 116, 118
Norton-Simon, 101

oak barrels, charred, 19, 22, 27, 28, 94
Old Boone Distillery, 118
Old Charter brand, 84, 97, 106
Old Crow brand, 43–44, 50, 53–54, 96
Old-Fashioned Copper (OFC) Distillery, 52, 69
Old Fitzgerald Bottled-in-Bond brand, 84, 99–100, 106
Old Forester brand, 57, 123–24
Old No. 7 brand (Tennessee), 107
Old Oscar Pepper Distillery, 42–43, 44, 54, 68–69
Old Overholt brand, 96
Old Quaker brand, 96
Old Rip Van Winkle brand, 118
Old Stagg brand, 96
Old Taylor brand, 52, 96
Oldtyme Distilling Corporation, 97
organized crime, 86–89
origin legends, 20–22, 24–26

Oscar Getz Museum of Whiskey History, 121–22
overproduction of whiskey, 68–69

packaging, 57–58, 70, 84, 109–10
Pacult, Paul, 118
Panic of 1873, 68
Pappy Van Winkle Family Reserve brand, 118
Paris and Allen firm, 53
Park and Tilford Co., 98
Parker, McWiley, 48
penicillin production, 102
Pennington Method, 6–7
Pepper, James E., 58, 61
Pepper, Oscar, 43
Prohibition, 77–90; criminal activity during, 86–89; economic effects of, 81–86; Eighteenth Amendment, 77, 81; opposition to, 52, 78–79, 89–90; temperance movement, 77–80; and World War I, 80–81
prohibition: Civil War, 48; World War I, 80–81
proof, 37, 42, 68, 94–95
proof gallon, 63–64, 65
public relations, 92
Pure Food and Drug Act (1906), 52, 73, 74–75

quality assurance, 56, 57, 88
Quebec Distillers, 98

railroad industry, 32–35
Rat Pack (entertainers), 107, 111
recipes, 6–11, 46–48, 93
rectifiers, 45–48, 67–68, 70–76, 79
Regan, Gary, 119–20
Regan, Mardee, 119–20
regulations: Bottled-in-Bond Act, 52, 70, 73–74, 83; bottled-in-bond legislation, 52, 70–74, 83;

139

regulations *(cont.)*
  bourbon as distinctive U.S. product, 110; and country of origin,
  56–57; Forand Bill, 105; licenses,
  15; Maine Laws, 77; post-Prohibition, 91–94, 111; Pure Food
  and Drug Act, 52, 73, 74–75;
  and taxation, 63–67; and trademark registration, 57; and trusts,
  69; Volstead Act, 81, 84, 89. *See
  also* Prohibition
Remus, George, 87–88
roller mills, 38
Roma Wines, 97
Ron Carioca Distillery, 98
Roosevelt, Franklin D., 90
Roosevelt, Theodore, 75
Rosenstiel, Louis, 102–3, 105
Russell, H. H., 78

Samuels, Bill, Sr., 107–8
Sanders, Lewis, 22
sanitation improvements, 42
Schenley Distilleries: closure of,
  81–82; effects of World War II,
  101–2, 103; expansion of, 111;
  marketing, 105–6, 107, 109,
  115–16; post-Prohibition, 95–98.
  See also I. W. Harper brand
Schenley Distillers Corporation,
  81–82
Schenley International Corpora-
  tion, 96
Scotch-Irish settlers, 20
Scotch whiskeys, 8, 113
Seagram Company, 95–96
Second Great Awakening, 77
settlers: distilling legends, 20–21
Seven Crown American brand, 96
Shapira brothers, 98
Sherman, William Tecumseh, 51
shipping industry, 31–34
Sinatra, Frank, 107, 111

single-barrel bourbons, 113
single-malt Scotch whiskeys, 113
Sixteenth Amendment, 86
small-batch bourbons, 116
sour mash, 7–9, 42
South Carolina Railroad, 32–33
speakeasies, 86
spelling variations, 13
Squibb Distillery, 96
stamps, taxation, 58, 61, 83
Standard Distilling and Distributing
  Co. of America, 69
Standards of Identity, 95
Star Hill Distillery, 108
start-up companies, 95, 98
steamboats, 31–32
steam mills, 38
stills, 3–5, 8, 36–38, 45, 52
Stitzel, A. Ph., 99
Stitzel, Frederick, 39
Stitzel-Weller Distillery, 85, 99–100,
  106, 118
straightbourbon.com, 123
straight whiskey, 70–76, 79, 94
strip stamps, 58, 61
superpremium bourbons, 113–19
sweet mash, 7–9
Swigert Distillery, 51–52

Taft, Alphonso, 73
Taft, William Howard, 75
Tarascon, John, 28
Tarascon, Louis, 28
taxation: early imposed taxes, 11–
  15, 26; federal income tax, 86;
  and regulation, 48, 63–67; with
  stamps, 58, 61, 83; during World
  War II, 104
tax collectors, 12–13
Taylor, E. H., Jr., 43–44, 50, 51–54,
  69
Taylor, Edmund, 73
Taylor, Edmund Haynes, 51

Index

Taylor, John, 51
Taylor, Richard, Jr., 51
Taylor, Zachary, 51
technological advances: Industrial Revolution, 36–44
temperance movement, 77–80
temperature regulation, 38–39, 42
Tennessee whiskey, 107
Three Feathers brand, 97
toasted barrels, 28
tourism, 121–22
transcontinental railroads, 34
trusts, 69
Twenty-first Amendment, 90

Uncas (steamboat), 34
United Distillers, 98
Urban Bourbon Trail, 122

Van Winkle, Julian, 82, 99–101, 118
Van Winkle, Julian, III, 118
Van Winkle, Julian, Jr., 118
Vietnam War: impact on industry, 110–11
Volstead Act (1919), 81, 84, 89

Walker, Hiram, 54, 56–57
Walker's Club brand, 54–57
Walsh, Glenn, 82
warehouses, 39–40, 66, 82–83
War Production Board, 101
Washington, George, 12, 14
water, limestone, 19, 42
Waterfill and Frazier brand, 84
Wathen Distillery, 103
Watterson, Henry, 79
Waymack, Mark, 119
websites, 122–23
Weller, Charles D., 48, 50
Weller, Daniel, 15
Weller, William LaRue, 15, 50
Weller Antique brand, 100

Weller Original Barrel Proof brand, 106
westward expansion, 3
whiskey: early recipes, 6–11; spelling variations, 13; taxes on, 11–15. *See also specific topics, e.g.,* distilling industry; Industrial Revolution; origin legends
Whiskey Rebellion, 12–15, 20
Whiskey Ring scandal (1875), 64–66
Whiskey Row, 35, 45, 51
WhiskyFest, 121
White Mills Distillery, 85
wholesale merchants, 45–48, 67–68, 70–76, 79
Wickersham Commission, 89
Wigle, Philip, 14
Wild Turkey brand, 119
Willard, Frances, 78
Willett Distillery, 123
Williams, Evan, 20–21
Wittenmyer, Annie, 78
W. L. Weller and Bro., 48
W. L. Weller and Sons (and brand), 82, 84, 99, 100
Women's Christian Temperance Union (WCTU), 75, 78, 79
women workers, 103
Woodward, George Washington, 50, 53
World Guide to Whiskey (Jackson), 119
World War I, 80–81
World War II, 101–4
worm, 4
wort, 8, 16

youth market, 111